THE AFRO-LONDON WAHALA

(Chronicles of an African Londoner)

By Marricke Kofi Gane

MarrickeGane

Publishing

DEDICATION

To everyone, who once lived in a land they didn't call home.

TABLE OF CONTENTS

INTRODUCTION

We Africans have many names we call London - the two that stick out most in my mind are *"London -The Leveller"* and *"Wahala-land."* The Leveller, because it is a general notion among us that London is no respecter of persons; it starts us all *(levels us all)* from scratch, no matter how much of a big shot we were back in Africa – unless of course you came hundreds of thousands or millions of Pounds rich. Wahala, on the other hand is an African *(Hausa)* pidgin word for trouble – used loosely. Yes, people remember the good things about London and the United Kingdom – but they also remember the *wahala* they experienced.

This book is about my own and other people's experiences in London, and other parts of the United Kingdom, told through my eyes. They are experiences Africans *(and other immigrants)* who have or still live in the UK, Europe, USA and other parts can identify with – it is our collective experiences.

Here is to reminiscing those first years of getting used to the *"Western way of life,"* and the quiet respites that follow, after we've been here long enough to start asking *"so what am I still doing here?"* Here is to our recollection of the light-hearted hustles, the disorientations, the culture shocks and everything else that made our migrant experiences worth remembering, worth sharing.

Things have and continue to change across Europe *(including UK)*, Asia, Australia, the Americas and even back home in Africa, but these experiences will continue to garnish the memories of everyone who travelled this road – past, present and future.

Whether you are, used to be or on the way to becoming an African Diasporan; whether in the UK, Europe, Americas, Australia or elsewhere; whether you know any, heard about us or simply curious about our experiences as Africans in the West – I hope this book makes you laugh, maybe sigh, nod, chuckle, shake your head, even shed a tear – whatever it makes you feel, that's your own wahala! Innit?

Marricke Kofi Gane

Author

CHAPTER 1

The Sniffer Dogs

It was December 2001, when the cold British air first clawed at my bones in Heathrow airport as I made my way off my British Airways flight. I had landed! The dream was suddenly a reality! To me, that first cold air on my face was more than just a cold slap – it was more like a *'welcome to your dreams'* salute especially aimed at me.

The flight was good – but it was the longest 6 hours I had ever experienced. It was the first time I had ever flown outside Africa, and as semi-ignorant as I was about the European experience, at intervals on the flight, I would terrify myself by pondering the unthinkable, *'what if the fuel runs out in mid-air?'.* Something kept gnawing at my typical superstitious mind that something must be out to prevent me from reaching the land of my dreams – supposedly. It didn't help that I was seated in a window-seat; my eyes were constantly scanning the wing for any signs of trouble. I wanted to be sure I could spot any danger before it happened – I think the many years of watching witchcraft-heavy Nollywood and Ghallywood movies had affected me more deeply than I thought.

As I went into the arrival terminal, I remembered what my friend Amu advised when he last spoke to me at Ghana's Kotoka international Airport – *"it's easy to feel out of place at first but just watch everybody else and do what they do"* and that's exactly what I did all the way through immigration. I observed what others were doing and followed suit. Amu had been here before so I trusted his advice and it had worked to perfection so far.

In my entire lifetime, I will never forget that stomach flipping moment I felt a tap on my right shoulder. I turned around and the first thing I noticed was the dog, then, the three airport policemen standing around me. I had picked up my luggage and was trying to read the directions I had been given. I was to be picked up and taken to my host's house in Thamesmead, South London. As for the first words the huge redhead policeman spoke, not even a medical procedure could erase that from my memory:

"Sir! Do you mind stepping over here with your luggage for a minute? Our dog here may have picked up a scent from your luggage and we need to check your bags."

Suddenly, the cooling breeze I had been experiencing turned into sweat on my face. My heart sank to my stomach and rose again, threatening to bring with it the last snack I ate on the flight. *"Jesus eeiisssh! What have I done?"* I had read and heard tales of travellers being caught with drugs and the like but it was the last thing I would have imagined, and I had none, but nevertheless, I felt fear grip my intestines. Had Kwabena, my best friend, who helped me pack, planted drugs in my bag? No, that was inconceivable, he was one month away from being ordained a reverend minister!

By now, my heart seemed to have left my chest cavity and was in free fall.

I was escorted to a cordoned off area, two men with gloves were ready, my passport and tickets were taken from me and then the questions started

"Can you confirm your name for us?" I was silent. I was having an out of body experience.

The stern bulky policeman exchanged a knowing glance with his colleague and tapped me on the shoulder again. It was as though he had magical powers, because anytime he tapped me, it jerked the life either in or out of me. Revived, I called out my name. How I managed to answer all their questions, I will never know.

The dog was brought around again, this time to the opened baggage and that's when it dawned on me. I pulled out a black polythene bag that had been duct-taped several times over. Almost immediately the light dawned. With barely disguised looks of disgust they prodded the package in my hands, asking

"What is this?"

"It is dry and salted tilapia fish sir."

Of course, they made me unwrap it. The stench overwhelmed us and as if remotely choreographed, all the officers stepped back. Momentarily, I felt I had scored a little victory, *"serves you right"*, I said to myself. *"What the bloody heck is that?"* one of the officers spluttered, still holding his nose. I was relieved the whole episode had allayed their drug-related suspicions and that I would not be thrown in jail before I had even left the airport.

I was warned about bringing foodstuffs into the UK but it wasn't necessary anymore. From that moment, I vowed - never again!

I have lived in the UK over fifteen years following that episode and hardly ever bring foodstuffs from Ghana to London, especially not as a favour for anyone. Yes, I do enjoy Ghanaian food in London, but believe me, when sniffer dogs get involved in the food chain you stand to lose more than just your appetite!

There was a funny side to this memory, however. I remember riding on a bus one early morning from Victoria station, heading down to South East London many years later. There were just two of us Africans on the bus – I had my backpack and the other African, a lady, had a couple of bags with airline tags on them. She had obviously just flown in from somewhere.

I looked at the faces of the white folks on the bus – the stench from the semi-dried salted fish was getting to them, wafted through the bus by a persistent dawn breeze, the stench was very pronounced. I knew I wasn't guilty – so it must be my pretty black sister. I wanted to laugh. I really did want to laugh out loud. By now she knew, she could see it on their faces and hear the whispered comments, but she was busying herself with her phone. I knew - she was not doing anything on the phone.

I knew she was sweating under her coat from embarrassment and wishing the bus would hurry her to her destination. No, she couldn't give up now, she and her fish were almost home, just a couple more stops to go!

You made it too, sister! I smiled to myself – I was in your shoes some years back. You beat the sniffer dogs, so hold on – you are almost home.

CHAPTER 2

Serve Me Proper Breakfast

I had known Mary in Ghana, before I left for the UK. After she shared her plans to come over to the United Kingdom, we thought through options around her arrival and I agreed to pick her up from the airport and take her to a distant aunt somewhere in Kent

Eventually, the day came and her flight arrived. I waited for thirty-five minutes before she came out through the doors. I had decided I would buy her breakfast but certainly not from any of the bars or diners at Heathrow airport. It was not that I couldn't afford it; it was just that I knew the same breakfast would be a lot cheaper away from the captive audience, that is the traveling public, and as a money conscious immigrant, I was always looking after the pennies.

Three or so miles into London, I stopped at a coffee shop a friend and I had once used, before telling Mary that it was a good place for her to grab some breakfast – *"my welcome treat"*, I said. She looked impressed. It was as though the waitress had been waiting just for us. I gave her my order before I even sat down; a cup of coffee and full English breakfast. I asked if I could help Mary make a choice but she indicated with a hand gesture that she knew what she wanted. With a smile she said serenely,

"Please, Milo."

I almost choked on my spontaneous laughter and had to stop myself from freaking out. The Eastern European waitress was looking puzzled. I asked her to give us a minute. I leaned over to Mary and explained to her that while I understood what she meant, not many people in greasy spoon cafes in London were likely to.

In Ghana and perhaps, Africa in general, Milo is a hot chocolate drink made popular by the Nestle brand. I explained to her the difference between *"Milo"* beloved in Africa and *"Tea"* beloved in Britain, hot chocolate and Lipton's Teabags, respectively.

"So, would you like to order a cup of hot chocolate, then?" I ventured. She nodded, a little embarrassed. Then, unsure if she had grasped the technicalities I asked,

"Do you want cream in it and toast with that?" she nodded eagerly, responding, *"Everything!"*

We talked about her flight and her plans now that she was in the UK, as we waited for our breakfast. Mary's breakfast arrived first, but something was wrong. The expression in her eyes said it all. She was clearly deeply disappointed. Was it the white foamy cream on top of the chocolate drink? *"You can scoop that bit off if you don't want it,"* I said helpfully, but she shook her head, it was obviously not that. The waitress was also looking concerned, worried that she had got something wrong with Mary's order.

Then, Mary spoke in our native language,

"Aah!" she said plaintively, *"I said I wanted everything so where is the Chibom?"* At this point I could contain my laughter no more – I laughed until I cried. The poor waitress smiled and walked away, even more confused. I finally got myself under control when I realised that my guest obviously did not see the joke.

Truth is, where we come from, cafes are not something we're very used to. What we tend to have are food vendors *(like hawkers)* who station their breakfast stalls on street corners and from whom the youth, workers, school children and the old, choose from their variety of breakfast servings. Traditionally, an order for tea or *"Milo"* from these street vendors came with *"Chibom"* – a thick, well fried 2 or 3-egg omelette stuffed into a foot-long bread.

Mary obviously thought that breakfast would be the same in the UK. But I couldn't blame her – after all, if street food vendors back home in Africa could offer portions of Chibom, from their meagre resources, how much more likely was a British café with kitchens and sitting space, able to offer the delicacy?

I laughed my heart out and eventually ordered a full English breakfast for her – yes, with everything: tomatoes, mushrooms, hash browns, eggs, sausages, bacon, toast, and the whole nine yards of everything that makes up an English breakfast. To give Mary her due, she gave this new breakfast fare a chance; she ate everything except the hash browns and bacon.

Welcome to Britain my sister, welcome.

CHAPTER 3

Old Roger is Alive

I lay flat on my bed, staring at the ceiling, hoping the confusion in my mind would disappear. It was the same feeling I experienced throughout my bus journey back home – but now with the benefit of seclusion, it was a much deeper feeling. Humbling and thought provoking – that's exactly what it was.

It was the first time I had decided to take a walk by the famous Thames River; the stretch that ran alongside Woolwich town centre, not very far from the Woolwich ferry landing. It's interesting that at that time, Woolwich was referred to as the *"Naija"* capital in Britain *("Naija" is the slang for Nigeria)*. There was decent sitting and skating space, created right in front of the river. I sat down to absorb it all. That was when Mr Ade struck up a conversation with me. Ade, as I later found out was a fellow West African, Nigerian to be precise, fifty-seven years old and living on social benefits.

"Are you Ghanaian?" he asked

"Actually, yes I am. How did you know?"

"Ah, I know now!" His Nigerian accent was obvious. I smiled back.

"Are you here to study or work?" (sounding like *"stordy"* and *"war-k"*) I hesitated. I was doing both but I wanted to sample his separate reactions so I responded:

"I am here for School"

"Eheeerh! That one is good, now. But my brother just make sure you go straight back to your country when you finish, eh?"

'Interesting' I thought to myself. It sounded more like a warning than anything else and whilst I was pondering, he added

"Don't end up like some of us, eh? I take God beg you" (translates as I beg you in the name of God)

I probed his grim warning and he offered me an hour of his unbelievable life story.

Like me, Mr Ade came to Britain very young, schooled and soon after, got a good job in the city. Then he got *"sucked"* into it all. The freedom he never had back in Africa, the lifestyle he longed for – it felt like now was the time, it was all or nothing. Back then as he put it, he lived for the day, but the days were adding up. The opportunity to spend on credit was intoxicating, so his credit cards were overused. He went for the latest home furnishings, cars, you name it. But even the cars came on hire purchase so it wasn't at all painful at the time, but the huge debt monster was hot on his heels.

All this time, he was still in touch with his folks back home in Nigeria. He recalls how he kept putting off pleas from his old mother, to build a house in Nigeria to serve as a *"fall-back"* if he decided to return home. While he agreed, it was a good idea, Mr Ade postponed making a start, month after month until sadly both his parents died in a tragic road accident.

Right after losing his parents, things started to go downhill for my new friend. His girlfriend left him, his cars and newly mort-gaged house got repossessed. Grimly, he recounted how he per-petuated his own demise by rationalising that with his parents gone, he had nothing to fight for and that was when his down-ward spiral intensified. Then he asked a rhetorical question that made me realise how critical and balanced a thinker he was.

"Isn't it ironic? It was as though their being alive was the reason for my success"

Both our heads were bowed, as we stared at the paved floor.

"But you have done well by allowing your experience to be a blessing to oth-ers; I mean, by helping me not to fall in the same trap." I offered.

Somehow, a part of me felt there was something missing about Ade's *"Nigerian-ness."* As a child, I lived in Nigeria for close to seven years, have Nigerian friends and even lived in a shared flat with a few. If there's one thing I find a mark of most Nigerians, it was this – they were forceful and resourceful. A people who hardly gave up on life, a people who always found a way around life's gripping moments or at least fall trying – they dare. But maybe that's just my observation – life, has its own way of mak-ing and unmaking us, if we let it.

As he stood and patted his trousers down, my own guilt rose in me by virtue of being a fellow African. It was painful to see a brother had lost his way home to Africa. I was convinced Ade was going to find neither the reason nor the strength to ever return to Nigeria, for fear of the shame of returning empty-handed.

To me, he had lost nothing, but himself – a lesson I am grateful I learned.

CHAPTER 4

Mind the Gap & Black Cabs

"*Where are you off to sir?*" asked the taxi driver.

"*Elephant*" To be honest I knew it was Elephant and "*something,*" I just couldn't quite remember "*the something.*" But I figured it was very popular, a taxi driver would know what I meant. I was armed with a piece of information I had received once about black cab drivers – they are required to know London very, very well. What I wasn't aware of however, was the fact that black cabs were the luxury end of the taxi ecosystem of London. Where I come from, taxis are taxis.

"*Do you mean elephant and castle?*"

"*Eheeeh!!! Yes! Yes! Yes! You know it, that's the one!*"

He could see I was excited that he had connected the dots of my enquiry. What he wasn't expecting, however, was me haggling over the price of my ride before I got in the cab. He went red in the face for a moment before realizing that I must be new in town.

"No, no, no - you pay when you arrive at your destination!" he explained patiently

"OK, let's go then," I said.

I jumped into the back of the taxi assuming the price was going to be very reasonable – just like it was in Africa. Even then, I had it in mind to haggle with him when we reached my destination – to me, it was normal.

Between Dartford and Blackheath, my attention was caught by a little number-counting box on the taxi dashboard that I later found out was the meter making a little *"ching"* sound as the miles added up. At first, I thought it was a clock.

Curious, I checked my watch.

It wasn't a clock.

Then I figured it was probably a countdown of the mileage to my destination – well, I was almost right except that when I finally asked the driver what it was, we were just going past New Cross Gate and he said,

"Oh, that is just adding up the fare, sir."

I looked to see how much I had accumulated so far, knowing very well I was on a shoestring budget and, having just arrived, had no concrete job.

"Jesus!!!" I had already clocked up £15.50. This was not happening! I only had £30 in my wallet and the budget around it was very tight.

"Excuse me, sir, did you say something?"

"Yes, please! Stop! Stop! Stop" I could see the confusion on his face, but that was the least of my worries right now.

"Is something wrong sir?"

"Yes, please. I forgot something so I must get out here. Yes."

"So, would you like me to drive you back to get it?"

"Nooooooo! No! No! I will just get off now."

I don't think it occurred to him my behaviour had anything to do with the fare – At least that was something; it would not add to the shame of biting off more than I could chew. I paid him what the fare was – ten years down the line, I still remember it to be £15.50. Just before I got out he called out to me.

"Please, do mind the gap!"

I didn't know what he meant. The only gap that was an immediate bother to me was the hole the ride had created in my weekly budget.

I found myself at London bridge underground station the evening of the same day. It was my first visit to the underground, and I had to wait for the Jubilee line train. It had been a successful sortie so far; I had cleared the ticket gates and found myself successfully on the platform.

Just as the train arrived, a voice crackled into life *'PLEASE MIND THE GAP between the platform and the train"* it warned.

17

"Ahhhh" I hesitated as I stood one leg on and one leg off the train. The phrase *"mind the gap"* was familiar. The taxi driver had said it earlier and after that experience I needed to be sure. So, I climbed back up to the ticket hall to check with a customer service agent, whether I had the right ticket to take me to my destination and that no nasty shocks were in store for me and my wallet when I arrived at the other end. After all, once bitten twice shy.

More than fifteen years later, it is clear to me now the only reason the black cab driver told me to *"mind the gap"* was because he had parked beside an open telephone culvert on the side of the pavement where I alighted. I had been so engrossed in the dent the ride caused my pocket, I literally took everything the cab driver said, to be a piece of clue to solving my £15.50 mystery at the time.

Now, every time I hear the phrase *"mind the gap"* at the London underground stations, I smile. I smile not at the gap between the train and the platform, no, I smile at the fact that a gap in my pocket, caused by an over-adventurous black cab ride was my first understanding of *"gaps"* in the UK.

I am sure you remember your own *"gap"* experiences.

CHAPTER 5

The Ways of Love and Other Things.

Before I came to London, I could confidently say I knew a thing or two about women, but *"London the Leveller"* always has its own way of addressing high egos. Suffice to say the events I became involved with, made me feel like I needed to go back to school all over again, at least where women were concerned.

I have never been quite sure if this is a cultural or male perspective to equality in societies but quite clearly, back in a large part of Africa, most women didn't have a voice – until recently *(glad it's all changing)*. In most cases, they couldn't say what they meant, couldn't mean what they said, let alone act out what they wanted. The contrast for me when I first came to the UK was sharp and stark – the laws of the land were supportive of women, women were more open about their lives, expectations, emotions and actions but even then, in the recesses of my mind, I still secretly thought some things remained the preserve of men, at least from the viewpoint of the culture I came from. One of these, was a man *"hits on a girl" (makes a move on a girl)*, not the other way around.

Amy broke my *"cultural virginity."* I met Amy in my first job as a Security Guard at a Sainsbury's in Dartford. I think I can describe Amy in one single word – WILD! Being an extrovert, she was the first to make friendly conversation and I gladly returned her banter. I must have been twenty-six at the time and she was in her early twenties. Somehow over the first four weeks she gradually managed to get her lunch break to sync with mine. I knew it was intentional because as guards we always took turns and mine, out of preference was the late lunch at 3pm by which time all the regular staff would have cleared the canteen. To cut a long story short, she gave me a baptism of fire – she asked me out one Saturday for a movie date after work and interestingly, she was so sure I would say yes that she had already bought the tickets.

I accepted her invitation and enjoyed it. Shocked? Yes, I was that she asked but I also understood very quickly that things were done somewhat differently in the UK. We ended up at the pub for some drinks. Trying hard not to disappoint, I downed a Guinness. I didn't usually drink because of my Christian faith, so as you can imagine, it only took the first glass of beer for me to start feeling tipsy. There were a few more outings that followed.

This particular day, was about the fifth time we were having a drink together after work and a few weeks since the last. I don't remember a lot but I do remember Amy certainly had a lot to ask me about Africa – she even dared ask how African men were like, sexually. I flushed. I ignored the question, unsure where she was going with it. I was quite shocked that she had gone there at all – that's certainly not a topic we would talk about in a public place back home. I thought to myself *"Ha! This country is very different."* Unwisely as on other occasions, I went ahead with a third pint of Guinness, the first two rounds had been on me and she insisted that she wanted to return the favour by buying the third – I obliged, after all it was free. With my glass half empty after her round, the only thing on my mind was the nagging question – *"how in the name of my Ancestors, was I going to get home?"*

We were laughing so hard that when I heard her ask *"will you make a baby with me Kofi?"* I FREAKED, almost choking on my laughter. For a split second my childhood fantasies came alive and I wished I had vanishing powers. I thought I had misheard her. In the over a decade since that night, I have never forgotten that moment.

I liken the scene to a typical Nigerian movie – the lead actor is sitting in his posh living room with a glass of brandy in his hand and then suddenly, he jumps across to the other end of the room on seeing a ghost of his ex-girlfriend mysteriously appear in front of him! That's exactly how I reacted. The fuzzy booze haze cleared instantly and noticing the shock on my face, Amy shocked me even further by laughing it off with a childish giggle.

"Aww! Look at you (giggles); look at the expression on your face, you are so cute!"

"Look, I see you are very uncomfortable – but hey, you have a think about it and let me know what you think, OK Kofi? (giggles again)"

Clearly, it was the African in me that was shocked to the core and perhaps also a bit of my Christian upbringing came into play too. Whatever it was, it certainly was, it shocked me well. Now, many years down the line, I laugh at myself when I reminisce. Back then I think the shock on my face scared the poor girl away, not the *"no"* I wasn't brave enough to say.

Today, I have come full circle and I do at least appreciate the fact that there was a positive outcome to that encounter - a realisation that in my view, the UK society was proactively progressive. Amy and I were free to say what we wanted or believed, free to refuse what another person offered and no one would judge the other's choices. To me, that is a progressive society.

Seven or so years after that incidence, I was to come face to face with what many may have heard about in other accounts. My then Zambian friend who was looking to regularize his residency via marriage finally found a European girl who agreed to marry him for convenience – a convenience that was negotiated at £4,000. That was a lot of money at the time. But as is the case with most of these *"citizenship operations"* – it can go well, or it can go very terribly wrong.

His went very wrong. Unlucky or foolish? It's hard to say when you are not in another man's shoes.

Joseph had secured his deal through a friend who had succeeded in his marriage of convenience, and that had been what convinced him to do it too. He had the confidence that it had worked for someone he knew. It all sounded like a very straight-forward process where there really was not a lot that could go wrong. In fact, The Home Office had not really started clamp-ing down on such marriages of convenience at the time, albeit it was still illegal if found. But of course, with such deals come certain requirements, and one of the main requirements is the ability to prove that the two persons concerned have known each other *"well"* over a certain period.

That's how it all started. Joseph moved in with his *"spouse of con-venience"* and lived there for about seven months, to make sure his mails and proof of address was aligned with hers, they got a few joint bills etc. After that, they got *"married."* The next step was for the couple to cohabit for another year or so. After that they could divorce by mutual consent and then voila!! – Joseph would have been a free man. Free to live in the UK. Well that is how it should have gone but in fact, it didn't quite go that way. Joseph claims his contract wife started demanding intimacy and if Joseph would not oblige she threatened blowing the whistle on the whole arrangement.

What was Joseph to do? He wasn't ready to be deported and he didn't come this far to back down. Again, I was not in his shoes so I could not say what would be the right or wrong thing to do in this situation. Some of his friends he sought advice from, simply said,

"Well, get on with it, what are you complaining about?"

But things took a turn, and what was meant to be a one-off intimacy resulted in him becoming a father of twin boys and his contract wife refusing him a divorce – not so straightforward after all!

There are probably much worse stories out there, and which-ever way we look at it, it's fair to say – *"the hustle is real."* I gained my British Citizenship through the Working Holiday Visa system, when it was in effect so, perhaps I will never know, but I have always asked myself, *"what would I have done if I was in Joseph's shoes?"* – thank God, I have long feet, his shoes wouldn't have fitted anyway.

CHAPTER 6

The Cleaner, The Guard, & The Brainiac

Before I landed in the UK, one of the misconceptions I had was that *"white folks were generally lazy"* – believe me, I have no idea how that notion was formed. It didn't take me more than a week after arriving in London to realize that the opposite was true. And after living in the UK for more than a decade and half, I don't only think the British are hardworking, I also think they are very efficient – obviously, that doesn't apply to *social-service-dependent* parasites. I mean, back where I came from, there was no such thing as being paid by the hour at a set rate. It meant that often, everybody was on a salary regardless of efficiency.

"Maybe" (and I did say Maybe), it's the reason why back in *"some"* parts of Africa people could take the day off, randomly to attend a funeral or other personal engagements, whereas here in the UK, if you didn't get a compassionate release from your supervisor then part of your annual leave had to be used and if you were working by the hour, then you'd earn nothing for those hours. Effectively in the UK, employers only pay for the efforts they get from employees and the latter only earn for

what they have delivered – a good part of unproductive hours, cut out.

An interesting thing I observed in my early years in the UK was the paradox where SOME Africans were happy to take on "*some*" jobs here, and for odd hours but wouldn't dream of doing the same in their home countries. For example, I worked with KK back in early 2004 – he was a cleaner. I have done many menial jobs myself before arriving at my current refinement. On a normal day, KK would do one cleaning job at 4am in Central London, run to a care-home in Bromley for a midmorning cleaning role at 10am and crown it with a long office complex cleaning job somewhere in Sutton from 6pm to 10pm. The cycle repeated itself every day with reduced attendances on Saturday and Sunday. But KK was happy to do it. Now KK and I once travelled back to our home country in Africa, and he NEVER told anyone what his real job was back in the UK. Oh no, that would have been a humiliation. Maybe it was an issue of creativity around the titles and maybe I was short sighted at the time in not appreciating the importance of keeping up appearances when one returns home to Africa. Truth be told, KK had gotten everybody to believe he worked as a *"Supervising Health Inspector"* back in the UK. When I found out about it, I beat myself up. Why hadn't I said that I was *"Director of Homeland Security?"* I was at the time still working as a security guard, which paid much better than KK's cleaning did. How the devil had I missed that trick?

But I suppose you could look at KK's position from different angles. On the one hand, it appears that in societies today, many are respected for what they have, not what they are or are capable of – so all KK had to do was, as we call it *"MELT"* his hard-saved Great British Pounds Sterling at huge rates and boom – he was a wealthy superstar at least for the time he was there on holidays. Another angle, is that many people's interpretation of how money matches status is quite simple – for example, this is how much KK makes in the UK in a month. If converted into local currency, it amounts to money that the local bank manager makes, so hey, KK's role as *"Supervising Health Inspector"* must be in the same league as a local Bank Manager, salary wise. That may not necessarily be far from the truth *(if KK's role was real),* and in the UK and many other western countries Africans migrate to, it creates a very strong temptation to remain in the low trenches, ignoring or even consciously downplaying the phenomenal opportunities these western economies present to us as economic migrants *(in most cases).*

I remember very well when I started my first ever job in the UK as a security guard – after the second or so month of work I accidentally found myself comparing my take-home pay to the take-home pay of my former work supervisor back in Africa. Shockingly I was earning a hundred pounds more than he did, monthly – yes, I was working a few more hours a week but gosh that felt more than good to know! And that's enough to keep most people in the trenches for a long, long time. Over time the rationalisation tends to be self-entrenching questions like: *"isn't the result all about what we all earn? So, if I am earning more…"* or you might hear others ask, *"If I should go through so many years of schooling and arrive at a salary still lower than a cleaner in the West, then to hell with further education."* The result, sadly, is self-stagnation.

After all, as a menial worker in a foreign land, I can build the same grand house, as a bank manager would back home. Sadly, for some, this is where the search for greener pastures ends.

Interestingly, it can be a paradox too. I have come across people, well read and who have plied their professional trades successfully, but who, in the latter analysis find they have nothing concrete to show for their labours – financially speaking. To many in this bracket, the consolation tends to be – *"well, my friends back home in Africa may have more than I have financially but I have more exposure and knowledge capital than they have."* It's hard to say what is of greater value – the money or the knowledge. You could certainly put forward the argument, *"Well, having knowledge, gives more potential to earn more money."* But you equally could put forward the argument *"money can buy you knowledge"*

All I am trying to say is this – no matter what level of education and knowledge one comes to the West with, there are phenomenal opportunities to add to it, multiply it, or even swap it, to add value to oneself. The choice is ours.

CHAPTER 7

The ATM Errors

Out here in the West, if you are an African and you haven't yet cracked the *"money code,"* in other words, if you are still *"hustling,"* the one thing you don't want to do is attempt to withdraw money in the daytime from an Automated Teller Machine *(ATM)*. Especially with a queue of people behind you, peering impatiently over your shoulder – and even more so, if you are not sure how much you have in your bank account.

I am certain quite a good number of us have experienced this. We may read and laugh about it now, but it was embarrassing when we first experienced it. You may, like me have had the experience of confidently walking up to an ATM, cockily slotting in your credit or debit card, not bothering to check the balance, then keying in the amount you wish to withdraw. You wait, possibly whistling a merry tune and then on the screen a message flashes in what seems like foot high letters: *"INSUFFICIENT FUNDS IN YOUR ACCOUNT"* or something similar – the singing stops.

At that point, you look round at the two people impatiently waiting behind you and that's when the cold sweat breaks out on your forehead. You try to ignore them and repeat the process, this time round, keying in a lower withdrawal amount. The machine takes a longer time to consider your new request but finally the same message flashes up on screen - *"INSUF-FICIENT FUNDS IN YOUR ACCOUNT"* – that's when you pull out your card, shamefaced and run off trying not to catch the disdainful eye of anyone behind you. Now the ATM prints out a receipt for your miserably failed transaction and then comes the humiliation, as a helpful soul runs after you shouting, *"Excuse me! You left your receipt"*

Usually one would avoid the ATM, any ATM and every ATM for the rest of the day. Closer to the end of the day, you might be tempted to quickly pop to another ATM to print a list of transactions showing all the moneys coming in and leaving the account. Six out of ten times, the cause of my own ATM embarrassment was a forgotten direct debit that had hit my account or in some cases, a series of them – yes, it does happen! Then, there is the misjudging of the date wages are expected to hit the bank account – and a forlorn attempt to get the payroll dates to sync with the time that money is needed. Or there are the times when you pay with your debit card for an expense earlier in a week and assume it cleared through your bank account, only to realise that it was hiding in cyber space ready to jump out and hit your account at just the same time you needed to withdraw some cash.

I was once in a bank queue when I overhead a fellow *"brother"* embroiled in an argument with the bank teller. The teller had told the gentleman that his account balance was reading zero and that information set off the brother – *"It is my account, you can't tell me that!"* he raged.

I empathized, I had been there before a year or so back when things, as we say, were very *"tight"* so I totally understood his frustration, albeit unfounded. Obviously, he was convinced beyond any doubt that there should be money in his account and so the polite teller's repeated, *"I am sorry sir, it's still showing a zero balance"* was just getting him more and more riled. His retrospective embarrassment would come later when he checked and realised the teller was right – maybe a direct debit he had forgotten had been taken from his account, or a payment into his account failed to show up when he expected it to. Whatever the cause, I know without any doubt, it wasn't the teller's fault; it never is!

Over time, I adopted the strategy of always locating an ATM nearest my place of residence and would creep out there at midnight to carry out all my transactions, free from the daytime audience.

What can I say? – the ATM never lies. It was never the ATM that got it wrong. Now we all know that, but back then, it was the easiest way to justify our frustrations about income miscalculations and erratic direct debits – *faulty ATMs. Really?*

Money, they say, makes the world go around – I say the lack of it, makes the head spin.

Like they say in Nigeria:

"Lack of money is lack of friends; if you have money, every dog in the village will claim to be related to you."

CHAPTER 8

The Big Red Bus...

Certainly, once you get a hang of it, public transportation in the UK is simple to use and effective enough to rely on – well, except when it snows. You can be sure most of your trains and buses will be on time. In fact, most bus stands and train stations provide information on transport arrival frequency or range of times within which to expect your transport. Now, there are Passenger Information Systems *(PIS)* at bus and train stations that tell you exact arrival and departure times. Outside of that, there are mobile Apps that do the same job these days – a few taps and your mobile application should be able to tell you when your next bus or train will show up, the route, traffic congestion spots and more. Effectively, you can plan your route, complete with estimated journey times even before you leave home.

To me, this was heaven. I am an extremely time-conscious person and even before I left my home country in Africa, I never quite came to grips with the phenomenon of *"African time"* – which is basically the discretionary time someone chooses as the interpretation of the clock time. So, the clock says 11.00am GMT or EST etc., African Time could be say 12.38pm or any time after 11.00am when one decides to show up or do what was originally scheduled for 11.00am.

But as a JJC in London *(JJC – Johnny Just Come)*, the first confusion with the public bus transport was the combination of 2 things – one, that all the buildings around me looked pretty much the same and secondly, all the buses and their bus stops looked the same. These two facts led to me being very, very disoriented for many days. Where I come from, buses may not all stop at a designated bussing point, but you can be guaranteed they will always shout out the names of all the destinations and stops the bus will make – and so often, you would know if it was headed in your direction. Believe you me, the bus may be on the opposite side of the road, but if the conductor is shouting a certain stop you need to be at, that bus will manoeuvre itself to that precise stop, one way or another. Just listen!

It might be that because I had mastered the art of functioning in complexity, simplicity felt odd and disorienting. Whatever the case was, I wasn't the only one coming from Africa who was thoroughly disoriented the first few days of attempting to use the bus system. I remember how, in my first two weeks, I would always find myself sitting on a bus and discovering, midway through the journey that I was going in the opposite direction to the way I wanted, although most bus stands had directional information.

On a few of those occasions, I'd doze off while the bus took me all the way to the last stop, only for me to realise that I was a long way from home or on the opposite side of town that I was hoping to get to.

Then, there was the irritation of waiting for the notorious bus number 180 from Belvedere that was always late and when it did eventually come, seemed to come in pairs – the late one and the on-time one! For some weird reason, this always happened when I was heading into town whereas in contrast, a more regular service operated on return journeys – *'how convenient,'* I always found myself chuckling.

And how could I have forgotten the occasional hundred-meter sprint to catch a bus, only to be within a hair's breadth of the doors as the driver pulled away – maybe, it's the reason we use the term *"catching a bus"*. Out of frustration, after heroic sprints, some frustrated travellers have banged at the doors, windows and back of London buses at one time or another – gosh I have even seen a frustrated lady take off her high heeled shoe and throw it, together with her handbag, at the bus. Yes, that's how desperate it gets. Me? I just punch the air or take it out on the neighbour's hedges or the bus shelter.

I have witnessed many crazy things in my time riding on London buses. I have seen people kissing, even going as far as daring a *steamy quickie* on the back seat of the top deck oblivious of the cameras installed on most buses. I have witnessed drunks vomit on innocent passengers, fistfights, telephone fights and dogfights. And oh, the drama queen mothers with their babies in buggies, youths boarding buses without valid tickets, a family of three smoking weed, bus drivers turning off the heating, passengers using the emergency buttons to open doors while buses are still in traffic, idiots turning up their music to deafening levels, fools urinating on the bus, a woman having a baby on the bus, foreigners getting lost on the bus, lost children found on the bus, Transport for London officers issuing offenders penalty charges on the bus. Yes, you can see all of life on the London bus system!

But of all these, not much scores higher for irritation in my view, than a loud, full-figured West African woman *(I won't name the exact country)*, having an argument over the telephone, in her local dialect. It is a known fact, that some tribes in African sound like they are having an argument even if just having a normal conversation. She was one of them!

But all in all, these vignettes of life are what make London bus rides interesting. To a large extent, you can almost always be guaranteed something interesting will happen on your bus ride – if it didn't, then you probably didn't ride on the Big Red Bus.

CHAPTER 9

The Afro-British Child Equation

I grew up in Africa. In fact, my childhood was largely spent running around West Africa with my father; from Ghana, through Liberia, Nigeria, Togo and back to Ghana and there's one thing I can tell you for a fact, at least back in the days circa 1974 to 1990s – *"they"* really bring you up *"disciplined!"*

Granted some homes were different from others but by and large, two things were very common about being brought up at that time – first, that era had the most varied collection of disciplinary tactics employed from the arsenal our parents had at their disposal. Secondly, if your own parents didn't discipline you, you still had a good chance someone in the immediate community would make it their personal business to take on the task.

I am sure some African brothers and sisters from that era reading this will remember the beatings with canes *(in fact, some parents, worked on the theory that treating the canes by soaking them in kerosene overnight, made them more painful on the skin)*; and who could forget the popular dried cow-tail called koboko, also used for lashing? How about fetching water for the whole compound, sleeping the night without dinner or kneeling in front of the family at dinner whilst they all ate. I knew of certain villages in which, if you were caught having sex before marriage or consenting age, you were guaranteed grounded wet pepper or ginger was going to be making the acquaintance of your private parts – and the way they put it was: *"it's not you being punished, it's the part of your body that misbehaved being corrected."* Crazy! I know. The list goes on and on.

Crude as it may sound – it kept us largely in line and doing *"wrong"* was not what you applied your creative thinking abilities to first and foremost – simplicita!! I remember growing up, all my dad had to do was stare at us and automatically, we were aware we had done something wrong and what corrective action needed to be taken– between my siblings and I, we called it *"the wicked look"* or better still *"eyes of steel."*

The examples are many but in hindsight now, I wonder, as am sure many others do, whether these, sometimes crude forms of disciplinary actions made us more timid than confident or perhaps even less daring than they did our heightened curiosity. Did they?

Raising children in the West is different, very different. I have kids, in fact, they were all born in London's St Thomas' Hospital and it's amazing the speed with which they gained confidence compared to how long it took me to utter my first reproving sentence in public. I remember taking my kids to London Zoo and the oldest one, only 5 at the time, had wandered off and started talking to some other parents and their children. When she returned, the African father in me pulled her aside to issue a fatherly warning:

"I think you should only speak to adult strangers when you have been spoken to, Otzara"

"Oh, don't be silly daddy, she doesn't mind" was her response.

I swallowed the lump in my throat and it was quite a lump. I thought to myself, if this were Africa, telling an adult not to be silly would be unthinkable. I know, she didn't say I was silly, but back home, you couldn't even use words like *silly, foolish, nonsense, idiot*, and the like in a conversation with an adult. The context never mattered – the fact it was coming from a minor was enough justification to get a smack across the face. Then you think about it and realise, indeed the world is changing fast and relying on one's knowledge alone was becoming a recipe for failure. The implication is that from a very early age, children must learn to network and connect with people on the go, and fast. That wasn't my daughter's thinking at the time, but having that understanding as an African father meant that what I would have considered inappropriate being brought up, had to be viewed differently in my children's era.

And once they started going to school, it was a whole new ball game. You know, in Africa, once your parents took you to school, learning was the prerogative of the teachers. At best after school, they would get you a private tutor to take you through a few more mental paces as extra-curricular activities. Two things I found different with raising children in Britain were: first, parents were required to be an integral part of children's learning process – especially in their early years. Secondly, education was holistic – children were expected to learn as much from nonacademic experiences as they would from the academic. It gets more intense when the children start *"demanding that engagement"* from you. I remember I had to be part of my two girls playing princess, cooking in their toy kitchen, hosting a puppet show *(I even had to pay imaginary money for entry, even though I worked to put up the show)*. I've crawled through tunnels in the park, acted like a monkey in their classroom – what can I say? It's humbling. It's so humbling I have been caught off guard several times at work singing songs and nursery rhymes at my desk. That's when you know it's starting to kick in: the kid-in-sanity! Oh, and I almost forgot the many birthday parties they had to attend because of invites from other children in their classes!

But again, it is also liberating to know that they are a step ahead in being confident to engage with the world, early. I have had numerous occasions when in the middle of intense running around, one of the children will simply stop and say, *"daddy I am feeling bored"* – that's when real creativity is called for, because I guarantee you they won't accept a game or activity they have already played.

Saying all that, however, there is something remarkable about African children and raising them in Britain or indeed anywhere else in the West – no matter how out of touch they may be physically with their African heritage, they someway, somehow intrinsically LOVE the taste of African food. My children had never been to Ghana when they first had a taste of corn dough porridge and Okra soup – *(Banku and Okra it is called)* – they licked their plates clean.

Here is what it comes down to for me, being an African British parent is an excellent opportunity for my children to have the best of both worlds – the rich cultural heritage of our African roots and the modernity of a globalised British society.

CHAPTER 10

Knock! Knock! Knock!

"*L*ittle pig, little pig, let me come in.*"

"No, no, not by the hair on my chinny chin chin."

"Then I'll huff, and I'll puff, and I'll blow your house down."

That's the story of the three little pigs and the big bad wolf.

Thankfully, houses in the UK are neither made of straws nor sticks – bricks. But when you are an immigrant in the UK, when you have overstayed your residency or share a house with someone who has, when your extended visa application is being processed at the home office, when you have borrowed money from the bank or credit card companies and missed a payment or two, when you have had an arranged marriage in order to regularise your immigration status or you're related to someone who has, when you are scared the CCTV cameras caught you going through a train station barrier without a ticket, or even if none of the above applies – it is probable that you, like many other immigrants would have considered an unexpected knock at your door, to be a big bad wolf. In the UK, as in many other Western countries everyone can be linked to an address, direct or indirect. Paradoxically, what is supposed to be the safest feeling, is also one of the scariest – the authorities know where you live. For most people, who come to the UK new, the first thing that crawls to mind at the sound of a knock on their door is *"what have I done to warrant being traced to my residence?"* Relax, it's probably just the postman.

One of the earliest paranoia I was infected with was – *"don't ever open the door if you are not expecting anyone."* The newbie that I was, I never quiet understood at the time. My host and I, were having a hearty chat in his living room two days after I landed when the doorbell rang. I rushed to get it only to be stopped midway and asked in a hush-hush, if I was expecting anyone. I was surprised, *"I just got here"* I mumbled. *"then don't open it"* he whispered. What followed, baffled me – I was shepherded to sit back in the sofa quietly, while he tiptoed upstairs to take a peep through the small toilet window, to establish who it was at the door. Whoever it was at the door on that fateful day has remained a mystery to me all these years – the door was never opened. Funny, I have done the same once or twice, many years after that experience. I wasn't lucky to have a storey floor, so, my peeking options were limited to the corner of my kitchen or bedroom window, or if one was daring enough, the peephole in the front door.

As I came to experience myself, there can be many reasons we immigrants would shudder answering knocks on our doors. Maybe it is to avoid a group of Jehovah Witness congregants who want to share their Christian tracts with you and have a conversation about their faith, or if you have met them in the past, they were probably back to follow up on whether you read the first tract they gave you, would like another, or are happy to come to church. Perhaps it is to avoid the folks from the disability, animal or international charities – a usually cheerful bunch, very tenacious at convincing you to sign up to monthly donations to save animals, or provide food, water or shelter to poor children in some remote part of a developing country. Having worked in the charity and development sector, these for me were the easiest to dismiss – I simply spewed out my thorough understanding of the nature of work their organisations did and round it off nicely with *"I work for XYZ and we fund a lot of your projects already."* But don't be fooled, some of them can be so persuasive, you almost feel inhuman for refusing to support their charitable causes. Then of course there are the researchers, poll and survey data collectors who come around from time to time collecting data for market, public or other research. With the advent of technology, these door-to-door data collectors have somewhat disappeared. These days, you either get survey requests via emails and texts, which are less intrusive and easier to respond to. Last in this category of less *"intense"* but somewhat unwelcome visitors, are political campaigners. Though seasonal, the irritation with this lot is merely the many political party representatives who each want to pitch to you for your vote.

In comes the *"intense"* and *"very unwelcome"* visitors that many immigrants will not open their doors to – not for all the potato chips in Britain. First on the list are Bailiffs. Most people I know, are petrified enough just receiving letters from bailiffs warning of possible visits, seizure of assets and property, to cover defaults on mortgages, loans and credit card borrowings. So, seeing these bailiffs physically on their doorsteps can for most people, feel like a meeting with *"fear-in-the-flesh"* – a terrifying reality. A friend once described her trepidation to me – *"Marricke, I don't know how to describe it, but it's like meeting death face to face and death saying 'Hello'."* I totally understand her.

Next, the Immigration Enforcement Officers – the greatest dread for any immigrant whose residency rights are expired. I used to ask myself of immigrants who fall to the immigration authorities, *"why stay here if your right to remain is expired, why don't you just go back home?"* That was me being naïve then. For some immigrants, that's like starving their entire village back where they came from. I used to have a friend whose trip to the UK for study, was sponsored by contributions from his entire village. For someone like that, he not only had to stay after his study, to work and pay back his due – he also had to make their investment in him render dividends. People have different motivations for being immigrants - many. Lex, my ex-colleague from Botswana said to me once *"Marricke, if we had our way, no one will like to leave their home countries you know."* Those back home, would argue *"but we are still living back home and making it."* I have been in both shoes and believe me, I understand to a good extent, the validity of both arguments.

But back to British Immigration Enforcement Officers. I once saw them in action and it was a mixed feeling – of admiration for their swift and tactile manoeuvrings and of grave pity for the immigrants they caught up with. It was a Wednesday in September 2013, I was out jogging around 5.30am. I knew the flats being raided very well – the ground floor of it was my favourite Chinese food shop and I was well acquainted with the couple who ran it. I suspect a tip-off informed the raid. The whole movie-style raid was done and dusted in 15 minutes from when I saw their vans circle the shop/flats, their entry, and marching out the poor immigrants who conceivably could not show immediate valid proof of residency. The couple were left behind, but the "*still sleepy mixed with fear and confusion*" looks on the faces of the three male and two female Asians marched into the waiting vans – that's a memory I can't ever forget. Three months down the line, the shop ceased operating. The reasons could be varied but my suspicions are that their staff were either prosecuted and deported or that the couple were heavily fined for using illegal immigrants.

Back when I first arrived in the UK, there were people who could get odd jobs without needing to prove their residency – that's all changed now. As at April 2017, employers face fines of up to £20,000 per illegal worker *(unlimited, if you knew about their residence ineligibility and still employed them)*, as well as criminal prosecution, a prison sentence *(of up to 5 years)*, and losing the right to employ migrant workers.

I am sure there are many other reasons why immigrants, African or otherwise will shudder to answer knocks on their doors but truth be told I think……..

Knock! Knock! Knock!……..someone's knocking on your door!!

CHAPTER 11

Being an Endangered Species

Before I came to Britain, I had heard stories of *"racism."* In part, I never quite got my head around why anyone would victimise another human purely because of their colour, but racism is what racism is – a psychological extension of a superiority complex, I suppose.

What I did find out coming to the United Kingdom was that racism came in different shades – perhaps it was even fair to say a thousand shades of grey. It doesn't make it any more acceptable, but it is worth knowing nonetheless, that it still exists, maybe not in the flagrantly brutal manner of centuries ago, or in the dark days of slavery or even recently as with the case of recent American police attacks on blacks. The lines, I must say, can be very thin between its various shades and the various ways racism is experienced. I experienced some of it in the form of attitudes, sometimes in the assumptions that directed people's interaction with me, other times as stereotypical interpretations of my thinking and actions - the different shades of grey are endless. Mine was on the mild end of the spectrum. Others may have experienced it in the mid-range and perhaps extreme ends of the spectrum for example in the case of the famous Stephen Lawrence murder.

A friend once did a class presentation in his London based university. In it, he started off by showing ten pairs of power-point slides of buildings, streets, airports, food, and the like. He explained to the class that for each pair of photos, one was taken in Africa and the other in Europe. He then asked the class to write down which of the images they thought was from Europe. According to him, about eighty per cent of the class were wrong, neatly demonstrating ignorance and or stereotypical assumptions about Africa. For a good number of persons in the United Kingdom, the closest they have come to any knowledge about Africa is the blacks they see or know or the images of war and starvation seen on TV.

Is Africa extinct? Physically, we are one of the most fertile and fastest growing populations globally, but with regards to our positive and progressive impact on the globe, we very rightly could be considered extinct. For now, that is until #AfricaRising fully kicks in.

I once travelled to a little town in UK's Lake District with a white girlfriend at the time. We had gone to visit her grandma in her huge farmhouse – apparently, she used to work for one of the UK's secret services and was now retired. It was refreshing, to once again see ducks and hens around the house, laying eggs all over the place. I was used to that in Africa and missed it in the artificial environment of London. Anyway, as we took a drive through the town on our way to the local Sainsbury grocery shop, it struck me. I hadn't seen any blacks. I dismissed the thought, thinking it was possibly because it was a Sunday and the weather, too cold for my black brothers and sisters to push a *'hustle'* in. I very clearly remembered visiting the village grocery shop – It still gives me goose bumps just remembering it. I walked behind my girlfriend into the busy fresh produce aisle, grabbed her by the waist and gave her a squeeze. That's when it felt like I was in a *"Bewitched"* movie – the whole aisle froze. Yes, I mean literally froze. You know how sometimes you feel someone's gaze on you and you just can't seem to shake it off? Multiply that by twenty or thirty pairs of eyes. My first re-action was to sample the expressions on the faces of my silent voyeurs. I was confused. I wasn't sure how to interpret their gazes – smiles, shock, and confusion - despicable me – again, several shades of grey. One thing that was sure about my un-certainty though was this – it all came down to two things, it was either because I was the only black kid on the block or that I was a black dude shockingly handling a white girl, and that's exactly where I left it. This wasn't, I reasoned, racism - perhaps ignorance or stereotypical assumptions about blacks was more at play here. Or was it? That's when I started asking – when does ignorance about the black race, if held for very long, start evolving into mild racism? Does it ever at all? Were the gazes, silent expressions of admiration, disgust or prejudice? Was a black guy like me allowed to be touching a white *"sister"* like that, especially in public? Or was it I who was being culturally insensitive?

On another occasion, I was traveling back from Durham, to my base in London and for the most part, it was a journey by train. At one of the countryside stops, a mother and her little son of about six years joined my carriage and sat on the adjacent seat. As is usually the case, we were all minding our own business except for the boy, who appeared quite intelligent I must say, pestering his mother with his incessant barrage of questions.

I like a curious mind, so from time to time I stole glances at them, giving the faintest wry smile and so did the old couple in the seat opposite mine. Now the mother was in a dilemma – she wanted to encourage her son's curiosity but also had to deal with any possible public nuisance he was causing. Then he dropped the bombshell – *"mummy, why is that man so dark?"* You should have seen the poor woman change from white to red in six seconds, and tell the young lad off, tears in her eyes.

For me, it was an opportunity – and I took it. I smiled reassuringly at the woman and told her not to worry, her son was a bright curious lad and his curiosity should be encouraged. All eyes were on me now as I moved over to sit opposite the little boy.

"Hey! My name is Kofi, what's yours?"

"Andrew" he responded shyly. He was unsure whether he had his mother's blessing to continue talking to me. She nodded at him, and you should have seen his face light up.

"Have you been on holiday before?"

"Yes!" he said enthusiastically, *"we went to Spain last year"*

"Well that sounds exciting; was it sunny, did you get a tan?"

He said he did and I saw an opportunity to explain to him I came from beautiful Africa and that down there, we are born naturally tanned. *"Cool"* he said, his eyes wide. Then I went on to talk to him about all the animals he had seen at the zoo and how they all exist in the wild in Africa. We were soon deep in conversation.

Sometimes, I must confess, pure ignorance of and about the black race can appear to have a racist feel to it and it takes quite a bit of discernment to separate the two. This was a child, and so it may seem harmless, but there are equally large numbers of adult Westerners who know almost nothing about Africa and Africans other than the occasional TV coverage of wars, starvation and disease they see, or Africans they see on the streets. For others, it's the few who appear in the jerseys of their favourite football clubs.

While we are at it, it may be worth laying out some hard truths. You see, back in Africa, a good percentage of the material we study in our educational systems, from archaeology to zoology comes from the Western world. In effect, upon graduation and now assuming a learned status, we have subconsciously also accepted that the knowledge of the West, and therefore the Westerner *(our knowledge benefactors)* is superior to us. What gives us power *(in this case, intellectual power)* must indeed be more powerful than we are. The lesser receives from the greater – that's right, isn't it?

But if Africa's *"own"* original knowledge, and the impactful propagation of such knowledge, was reaching the rest of the world, if our African knowledge was being applied globally and their applications were producing positive and progressive results globally, would Africa and Africans be perceived differently? If our own histories were written and told by us, through mediums controlled by us, would the view on Africa have been different? If indeed, our leaders were politically cunning, intellectually patriotic, domestically progressive and diplomatically ruthless, would the story of Africa have been different? And if we, as African citizens were all proud to defend her, sacrifice for her and see good in her no matter what – would Africa have been a different story in the eyes of the world?

Would we have been an endangered or the dominant species on the global stage, if we gave the world enough reasons to always stop, and listen to what we had to say?

CHAPTER 12

Civilizing the African Me

As a full-blooded African in the UK for the first time, I tell you, being *"Civilized"* according to British standards can feel like an *"unsupervised imprisonment."* There are so many things you can and cannot do that are materially different to the way things are done in Africa. I know some of you remember, and perhaps you cannot now accept the *"African way"* and that's fine – I am merely reminiscing.

But in part, it makes you wonder, doesn't it? – Who sets the standards and discriminatory behaviour principles for what constitutes being civilized or not?

I agree some standards are necessary for living a much more disciplined life and engaging the larger global society on an easily comparable basis, but there are still so called *"principles of the civilised"* that neither add or take away from you and some that are downright discriminatory towards our own unique culture.

Fascinatingly, there's one thing I have come to notice as an African adjusting to the so called *"civilized"* and etiquette lifestyle in London and UK as a whole – one quickly learns to live two sets of lives. The civilized life around traditional British folk and in public, and the unadulterated African life, lived in private and around kindred Africans. It may sound weird but I have come across brothers and sisters from Africa who will be on time for work, professional and public meetings and the like, yet invite them for a private, largely African event and they will surely turn up late – well, using the African meridian time *(AMT)* which incidentally ranges anything between GMT+0.5 to GMT+3.

I have a very good friend with very regular sinus itch, and I think a lot of Africans have sinus itches from time to time. The traditional African approach to dealing with it is largely twofold, or at least these are the two popular remedies – one option is to insert your index finger in the ear closest to the sinus itch and shake it vigorously until the vibration stops the itch. Alternatively, one could snort, by using short and noisy vibrations in the throat – until those internal vibrations stop the itching.

In fact, from experience, doing both simultaneously not only ensures an immediate relief – it is also highly pleasurable. Are these two culturally civilized remedies for an African in Britain? Well, I guarantee you two things – you won't find us doing it in public, but we will gleefully do it at home or in our cars *(with the windows rolled up of course)*, even if it means causing an earthquake.

Another friend with the same chronic sinus itching, keeps ear buds in her bathroom and handbags; in her bedroom however, she keeps a superior tool for its relief – a chicken's feather with its vane peeled off leaving just a small part at the tip. Its use can be ecstatic and intensely orgasmic – but I doubt if Africans familiar with it would use it in public or in front of their British friends, even in private.

As refined as I am, the African in me is still fascinated with a tinge of irritation when I see *"my people"* trying to eat certain African dishes with cutlery. The fascination is that it looks clumsy no matter how hard one tries and the irritation is that the same folks will likely just eat the same dish with their fingers at home so why not in public. I understand perfectly, they want to act *"civilized"* but truth be told, no matter how diplomatic one is, there are some African dishes you simply cannot be politically correct about by using a cutlery – you must use your fingers.

In fact, I dare say using cutlery on them makes one appear un-civilized. Imagine all the semi-solid African porridges made from corn or cassava flour? Imagine the popular African dishes made from pounding yam, cassava, plantains, cocoyam, and you name it. I cannot for the life of me, conceive the idea of *"demol-ishing"* them with a fork, spoon and knife. The way I see it, the five fingers of the hand each spell a cutlery item: S-P-O-O-N. Many fellow Africans are quick to justify why they must use cutlery on certain African foods - *"when in Rome, do as the Romans do."* My response usually tends to be a question: *"do the Romans eat matoke, or eba, or pounded yam, or banku, or aseeda, or injera, or pap?"*

There are many things, cultural or otherwise that Africans hold back on, simply because they want to appear *"civilised"* – we throw out our traditional clothes for the suit, tie and long dress-es; we throw away our plaited hairs for weaves and wigs; we undergo surgical operations to remove our tribal marks; we stress ourselves trying to hide our accents to appear *'posh'*.

I could go on and on but I suppose it all begs the much bigger question – what exactly fuels this desire to appear Westernized? Is it a misunderstanding that we cannot fit into a globally diverse society even with our unique cultures and that we can in fact do so not having to trade in what makes us unique? Or does the eagerness to shun our unique identities camouflage our hidden desire to run away from associating with a continent we feel ashamed of, for underachieving?

What is it that makes us much more assertive about other people's cultures and embarrassed about ours under the guise of being refined and civilized? What really, is being civilized if you think about it? Is anything the African ever does ever considered *"civilized"* – why not?

CHAPTER 13

Salvation: The Chippy and Coin Bank

I came to Britain in the winter. I know, right?

As I stepped off the British Airways plane and the cold winter air hit me in the face, I literally turned around wanting to scream *"Oh Jesus."* I remember the brunette hostess who was standing in front of the pilots' cabin to bid passengers goodbye seeing the desperation on my face and asking, *"did you forget something sir?"*

I smiled and suddenly, it dawned on me as the saying goes – *"forward ever, backward never."* I had to face it, cold or no cold – London, here I am.

After two or so months living between my host's house by night and the job centre by day, I got a job as a security guard. I worked for another four months, saved some money and decided it was time to move out and set up on my own. By this time, I was already missing my home country terribly. Calling my folks back home only made it harder – especially when all that my mother ever talked about was how she had made my favourite food two weeks ago and how this week was going to be my brother's favourite food. The weather was not a worry to me – but I missed my food. I missed the porridges, the okra soup, the cow-foot, pork and goat meats, everything that makes African food what it is.

Sadly, my employer lost a contract on one of our big sites and it meant our hours of work had to be rationed. My allocated times of work were so odd I couldn't even take on another side-job to help me *"balance the books."* I had to accept a drop in my wages without a corresponding cut in the cost of my rent. Something else would have to be squeezed. Suddenly I felt like the Exchequer of the UK Treasury trying to manage an entire economy – the African migrant economic crises.

I remember spending some days in my room praying. Funny as it may sound, Britain is one of those countries where you need an extra dose of faith, otherwise, it is easy to change your belief and believe that this is NOT one of the countries where miracles happen – you either work with the system and get re-sults or you let the system get the better of you. It's an interest-ing environment in my view – it rewards those who work smart and efficiently and punishes those who simply try to work hard, not smart, or both. The good thing however is that it is a system that forces you never to end your faith with just prayer. It is a system that quickly helps a typical African Christian immigrant realise this brutally obvious truth – as soon as you get off your knees praying, you need to apply your hands and brains.

So, as the finance minister of my own hustler economy, I re-solved to adopt a few austerity measures and massive cuts in personal spending and that included food. That's when the fish and chips and Chinese food shops in the high street caught my attention – they were going to be my strategic partners in the interim austerity period. Mr Val, the chip shop owner-operator became my buddy and I, his number one customer and rightly so – after all, I was there almost every day. So regular were my visits that Val knew what time to expect me and knew exactly how I liked my chicken, or fish. If it was chicken, it had to be one drumstick with the skin peeled off and one chicken breast with the skin left on, with the large cut potato chips of course. If it was fish, it had to be the tail end of the cod if it wasn't a full cod.

We ended up good friends, which meant that on good days, Val put extra portions of chicken or chips in my box. I even remember a few times when he gave me whole meals for free.

I was warned, when I first came to the UK, about the dangers to one's health of eating a diet of chicken, fish and chips from the corner shop. I suppose they were right, considering its processing largely involves deep frying in oil. For me however, and, I am sure for many who remember the experience of having to cut down on spending, the chicken and chips shop was a saviour, an ally more than a foe.

If you consider at the time, that between £1 and £2, was all you needed, to get a full satisfying meal at the chicken and chip shop – then you will understand that to some citizens, immigrants and professional hustlers the chicken and chips shop is almost a religious shrine – one worthy of their unswerving devotion. The reasons were simple – the chicken and chips shops were mainly just around the corner, they were very affordable and to some extent offered variety between chicken, fish and ribs. I have friends who at one point or another when things got very *"tight"* could survive on just the chips from the chip shop.

One way or another, it is fair to say the chip shop has been a *"strategic partner"* of choice in the austerity plans of many African immigrants. Yes, you may have the occasional lamb donner, or a Chinese takeaway but the chippy tops them all when the going gets tough. Oh! And how could I have talked about the chip shop without mentioning the bucket of coppers and coins we keep stashed away somewhere out of reach until those *"real hustle"* moments come to call. That's when we see the real value of those coppers and coins that we stashed away for a rainy day.

Believe me when I say; if you've been through those times, you will understand in a much deeper way, what the grocery giant TESCO means when it says:

"Every little helps" – yes! Every little does help.

CHAPTER 14

The Joys of Living in
A House-Share

When I first moved out of my host's home to live on my own in Abbeywood in South East London, I moved to a rented room in a house share. It wasn't the first time I had lived on my own although it was the first time in the UK and though it appeared a mundane event, for many reasons, as a grown man – it really felt like freedom. My own space.

My room was a converted living room of an original 3-bedroom terraced house now a 5-bedroomed multi-occupancy accommodation. I remember when I finally dropped off my last piece of luggage in my new bedsit, I lay on the bed, staring at the ceiling and blurted out the famous words from Martin Luther King's freedom speech:

"Free at last! Free at last! Thank God Almighty, we're free at last"

My housemates, one each, Ghanaian, Nigerian, Zambian and Namibian – a few more rooms and we could easily have made up a version of the African Union *(AU)*, but believe me the five of us were enough to ensure one drama or the other kept the house lively. Too lively sometimes, I didn't feel like going back home, then at other times, it was lively enough for me not to want to be anywhere else but home. I found out in most house-shares, tenants usually try to mind their business and stay out of each other's way. The mind set usually is *"we just share a house – I don't want to share your life."* I suppose in my new home, that was always at the back of our minds but then again, the Africans in us could not stay quiet for long. We simply thrive on community and interaction. Like they say, *"you can take the man out of Africa but you can't take Africa out of the man."*

If you have never lived in a house share in the UK, one of the realities that hits you the morning of the day after you move in, is the queue for the bathroom and the toilet. Of course, if you are the type who likes to take your time in the toilet every morning to transact your *"personal poo-poo business,"* you may have to either revise that comfort or find a new ritual. If you are unlucky not to have a separate toilet and bathroom it could really endanger your early morning *"personal business."* Either the waiting queue will pressure you to be done early, or you'll be driven to your wits end if the loo occupant before you took too long. Either way, mornings in a house share can be a real *wahala*. And how can I forget to mention that there are times you get to the bath or shower and the state it is left in by another housemate just makes you wonder whether a travelling camel or a working donkey had been bathed there the day before, but hey, it's all part of the joys of living in a house share.

Then comes the smelly foods and disappearing rations. I mean, it's a lot easier to deal with the smell of our foods if you are all Africans, as was in my case – it's a lot more difficult if the house share is made up of Caucasians and Africans. Don't get me wrong; Africa is a land of great food, natural food. Unlike others who stock their cupboards and fridges with canned or bottled foods, we are more likely to go with fresh foods. And when it comes to cooking them – it can become a whole carnival of mysterious scents. Yes, scents that are original, strong, natural and unadulterated. No, we don't bake our meat or fish – we steam or fry it and that comes with its unique scents. We don't eat our corn in the form of cereals and corn-on-the-cob – rather, we mill it, ferment it and cook it as porridge and that has its own unique smell.

The variety of food and combinations are endless, however, when people talk about African food being *smelly*, there are usually two culprits that comes down to – dried or semi-dried salted meat or fish and fermented corn or cassava. These two could very easily account for sixty per cent of the smell of African food that non-Africans find irritatingly stinky. To Africans however, these scents are nothing but heavenly – it's natural to us. I have met Africans, kids and adults alike, born in the UK but who, on tasting traditional African food for the first time, know that there's no turning back. It's a shame however that we Africans haven't done too well with making our indigenous culinary delicacies a part of British culture in the way the Chinese and Indians have.

Final stop – shagging next door. Yes, *"shagging"* is the British urban term for *"sex"* and there's nothing more annoying than being single, lying on your bed thinking about how you are going to feed yourself the following week and all you can hear is the bed upstairs creaking the hell out of the roof you were staring at for ideas and a woman screaming ecstatically *"Oh, Alex, you are a real man."*

As if that wasn't enough, guess what else? It turns out she was the only girl among us five tenants, and her boyfriend comes over on the weekends and Wednesdays, does his thing and leaves. What a miserable lot – yes, I know. But Mara *(not her real name)* never really cared much how we felt about her noisy shagging sessions. As far as she was concerned, she was an adult, living a perfectly normal adult life and we could go hang if we had a problem with it. And she was right, after all no one was stopping us from having girlfriends and joining the mid-week and weekend sessions.

I felt sorry for Martin *(not his real name)* the most. He shared the ground floor with me – Mara's room was directly above his, so he experienced the full impact of the creaking bed the most, while Sonni and Yamasi *(not their real names)* bore the brunt of Mara's ecstatic screams as their bedrooms both shared walls with hers upstairs.

Until I moved out of the property a year later, one truth was evident where *"shagging"* in our shared house was concerned – *"Alex was the only real man,"* the rest of us were watchmen, spectators and at best, absorbers of noise. I salute all those who go through the sometimes-torturous ordeal of being the *"sound engineers"* during their flatmates' shagging sessions. Quite frankly, I don't know what is more irritating – hearing them shag their brains out or being forced to smile and be nice to your flatmate's partner when s/he walks around the house smugly afterwards.

Oh well! It is what it is – the joys of a flatshare, *"innit?"*

CHAPTER 15

Professional Trick or Treat

In London, you learn very quickly that unless your work experience in Africa was with an international company with a strong presence in the UK, then any other experience is going to be heavily discounted. Sadly, our work ethics in Africa such as timekeeping, performance measurement and productivity issues *(at the time)* didn't help very much in the global perception of our capabilities – truth be told, many will agree it often seems like you must go the extra mile over and above, to be valued on a par with everybody else. That's all changing now however, with more international companies moving into Africa and making strides in enforcing their global operational standards in the African workplace.

So, I started as a security guard even though I had landed in the UK, a fully qualified Chartered Certified Accountant. At the time, and for an immigrant, the rates and hours available to work were all good – this was in the late 1990s to mid-2000s. In fact, rather than an immediate career mind set, the tendency is to think in terms of the wages and to make comparisons with salaries back home in Africa. And this is the same whether you find yourself working as a security guard, a bus conductor, a cleaner, a care worker, nurse, garbage collector, store checkout assistant, parking ticket attendant, factory worker, construction site worker etc. Until 2014 and beyond when residence-status immigration laws became very strict, these were the low profile, less conspicuous jobs that most Africans would hide behind – as launch pads for more ambitious ones and equally, they became final resting places for the less ambitious among us.

In fact, as a security guard, I remember one of the first things I did was to convert my first month's total pay into the local currency of Ghana, and to my surprise, I wasn't only earning more than I was paid back home – I was earning more than one of my directors back home! This temporary and magical *"wage-illusion"* is how many get their otherwise promising career prospects hijacked. It usually starts with the notion, *"this is a temporary job and it's paying OK. Let me make as much as I can for one or two years, then hopefully I can get a job in my area of professional expertise."*

That often turns out to be a steel trap, I have come to find out.

That one-year turns into two, then three, then four. I can hear you now asking, *"Well, why don't you just switched jobs?"* Well, usually your rent and other bills constantly need to be paid and as such, they force you to simply keep going, hardly giving you time to stop, THINK and take the necessary bold steps. If you are determined, then you will save and make the switch.

And here is something else that doesn't cross most people's minds once they get locked into the daily grind of the rat race – the only experience you will have to show on your resume at the end of those two, three or four years, is one from your role as a security guard, a bus conductor, a cleaner, a care worker, nurse, garbage collector, store checkout assistant, parking ticket attendant, factory worker, construction site worker etc. – it will be difficult to get onto the professional ladder with that. I was lucky I saw this trap very early on. I saved as much as I could over the one or two years that I worked as a security guard then I stopped, took a few practical courses in accounting again, and launched an intensive four months job-hunting campaign to find work in my field of professional expertise – accounting. When I got my first break, I gave it my all because there really was only one alternative – going back to security work. Just about the same time I got my first job as an accountant with an international charity, I had run out of saved funds and it would be a whole month before I got paid in my new job –another reason for many to stick with the weekly wage. Luckily, I still had my security guard licence, so I took a night security job for two months, meaning I would work in my career 9.00am to 5.00pm job in the day, get home at 6.00pm, and by 9.00pm, I was out as a security guard working from 10.00pm at night to 4.00am in the morning and back to my day job at 9.00am the same morning. Yes, you guessed right – my morning bus rides and afternoon lunches were my sleep periods.

My American friends put it best when they say – *"the hustle is real my hommie"*

Was it all worth it? Yes, it was more than worth the temporary sacrifice. Today, I have a well-built career and it may surprise you to know the hard work I put into that first professional role paid me back in more ways than just serving as a career launch – the employer was so impressed, when a change in my immigration status was due, they supported me in the transition to a semi-permanent status, paid for some of my professional courses and even gave me a glowing reference that boosted my career prospects when I left them.

If there's one thing I like to say to my fellow Africans who come into the UK or indeed any other Western country seeking greener prospects, it is this – the surest way to secure those prospects long-term is to do what most people never consider a priority beyond the *"money"* and it is this: recognise that the West offers tremendously varied opportunities to add value to yourself whether it is by going back to school to add a degree or professional certification to your already existing experience or qualification, or better still, allowing you to immerse yourself in as many available career targeted short courses, as possible. At the end of the day, it is the role-specific value you have and can prove, that employers want to pay you for – nothing more, nothing less.

If a professional career is not your thing, you don't need to miss out. The UK and most Western countries are very entrepreneur focused and you will find many government agencies responsible for small businesses offering comprehensive information about how to start a business. If you research well enough, you might even find support on finances whether publicly, government guaranteed or privately, for such entrepreneurial escapades – you just have to look and be daring to be rewarded.

I came to the UK as a newly Chartered Accountant. I worked as a security guard in my first job, even did a bit of cleaning work, construction, social care work of some sorts. Today, I have authored ten books merely out of my love for writing. Professionally I work as an International Development Fund manager, employing my accounting skills to manage large development funds on behalf of the British and other Western Governments. My first fund was just £50 million. After that, £200million and £500 million funds respectively, spread over 40+ countries around the world. My job has seen me work in some of the most life-changing environments like DR Congo, South Sudan, Mozambique, Rwanda, all over Africa and some parts of Asia. I started where most people start when they arrive in the UK – whether one goes on to build a greater value with themselves or not – that's always a matter of choice.

It's not all about the money – it's everything about the value we offer. One thing we must vow never to do, is to lose our professional and talent prospects simply because we allowed temporary *"survival"* to take over our entire lives. It must never happen.

CHAPTER 16

Jollof Rice Wars in the UK

West Africans love their food and their football. Food-wise, a dish that is common through most of West Africa is Jollof rice. It is also called *"Benachin"* in the original language of the *"Wolof"* people who originally hail from North Western Senegal and Gambia. Tradition has it that the Wolof people, rather than cooking rice and a sauce separately to go with it, would usually cook the sauce and rice together in the same pot. Families and communities would eat it from the same pot to instil communal unity. It is a paradox that around 2014 Jollof wars ensued among the different West African representations in UK.

Jollof is enjoyed in different variations in Gambia, Ghana, Mali, Nigeria, Ivory Coast, Benin, Togo, Sierra Leone, Liberia and Cameroon – all in West Africa.

How is it made? Well, various versions exist and within those versions, there are further variations. It shouldn't come as surprise then, that there may be hundreds of recipes out there for *"Jollof rice."* The basic elements however are tomato paste, onions, scotch pepper, vegetable oil and, of course, rice. As for the various permutations that ensue from that – heaven only knows. In fact, I hear in some cultures it is considered sacrilege to cook the dish with anything other than meat. I personally have eaten it with different sorts of meat as well as fish and eggs, but I find I like it best cooked with meat from start to finish. That's just me, but you can imagine the many millions of Africans and they all have preferences around the humble dish called Jollof.

Anyway, in the summer of 2014, Britain's top celebrity chef Jamie Oliver, on one of his shows, and in a post on his website, angered the gods of Jollof and the league of West Africans in and outside of the UK who descended on him like a tsunami. Jamie had published his version of Jollof, complete with coriander, parsley and a lemon wedge. To be fair, he did mention on his website that he knew there were different versions of the dish and that what he published was his version. Alas, it was too late the gods were angry and in the following few weeks following, the anger and ranting poured out in headlines and on social media.

West Africans felt their sacred dish had been defiled in more ways than one. And contrary to what many people thought at the time, Jamie's crime was not just a single transgression.

Jamie was considered an outsider and as such, was not knowledgeable enough to be an authority on the subject of Jollof rice. And although Jamie did not claim to be an authority, his celebrity and perhaps larger than life status implied his authority in cooking - and in cooking Jollof rice. That was his first crime and it is very possible it was not even a crime he realised he had committed.

Then there was the second major crime - the ingredients he used. To many West Africans it was out of order to have coriander, parsley and lemon wedges anywhere near Jollof rice – it was like dressing up a military head of state in G-strings, a pink bra and putting him on display complete with a feather duster in his right hand.

Finally, Jamie's attempts to show the dish as one that was quick and easy to make was perceived as denying the dish the love and care that should go into making it. To be fair, some folks will start preparing for the dish well over a day before it is cooked and eaten – now that's passion.

Jamie Oliver was just one Jollof transgressor. I suppose after he had been well and truly put in his place, people looked for a new argument and it wasn't too difficult to find one in the rivalry between the Nigerians and Ghanaians as to which country's Jollof was best. Considering the different African countries represented in the UK, there were comparatively few from Gambia, Mali, Togo, Sierra Leone, Liberia, Ivory Coast, Benin and Cameroon, so it made perfect sense that the Jollof war began between the Nigerians and Ghanaians – the two populous West African representations in London at least. As to who won, it is still debatable. In my opinion, this is not a war that anyone could win, neither is it a war that would ever stop and the reason is simple.

Throughout history, Nigerians and Ghanaians have always had a rivalry on everything and that came to a head in the early 1980's when Ghanaians living in Nigeria were asked to leave and return to their country – I was in Nigeria as a young Ghanaian child at the time, my father being an Engineer and I, in a school full of Ghanaian teachers. Way back then, I still remember vividly the anger-fuelled assertions, that Ghanaian teachers were better than Nigerian teachers, then it shifted to their respective national football teams and after that – the rivalry knew no bounds. Jollof rice was certainly not the first battleground, and it won't be the last - that's a fact.

If you ever find yourself anywhere with Nigerians and Ghanaians together, make sure any phrase or sentence you utter with Nigeria and Ghana in it, doesn't also have the words; Jollof, football, corruption or *"Ghana-must-go"* in it – you may very well be starting a world war.

CHAPTER 17

Soft Driver, Hard Driver

B ack home on a holiday, someone who also used to live in London told me – she never really understood how I managed to be the most serene and calm driver in London but a *"tough cookie"* anytime I came home to visit. I just smiled. Back in Africa, commercial drivers of taxis and buses were, and probably still are, known to be some of the most reckless of drivers, whereas the opposite is true of their counterparts in London. I was first taught how to drive by a commercial taxi driver in my home country and with that came the lessons of how to be a *"tough cookie"* on the road. I learned, when I arrived in the UK, that half of what I considered as being *"tough"* as a driver, was known in the UK as *"road rage"* – yep! How disappointing, sarcastically speaking.

So, for a long while since my arrival, and passing my driving test first time, I have often pondered – what is it exactly that makes a rough driver like me back home, an *"angel"* on the road, when driving in London and across the UK? The same driving rules we have back home apply here in the UK too. In my view, the only reason they work so well in the UK is this – they are enforced to the letter. It was an eye opener for me here in the UK, that *"indiscipline"* of any form, was a huge source of revenue for most local councils and boroughs. In some of these local government areas, punishing traffic indiscipline of one sort or another, was their largest income generation source.

I have come to accept, that the driving I had been used to in Africa and which was considered cool or normal was a no-no, and even ruled offensive under some of the traffic laws in the UK. I remember back home, it was okay to use the car horn at will for almost anything – to say hello to nice girls walking by, to greet my neighbours when I drove in my local community, to register my disapproval of something I saw by the roadside even if it was none of my business. Heck, I even tooted my horn when overtaking another vehicle one full lane apart on a dual carriageway – just so they were aware I had overtaken them.

That all changed when I arrived in the UK. At the time of writing, I have lived in London over fifteen years and I can tell you the exact number of times and the places I have had to toot my car horn – that's how few it is. I even feel deprived when I think about it sometimes.

I remember two incidences that shaped up my full and undivided adherence to motoring rules. In the first, I had gone for a holiday back home in Africa. I forgot I had opted for my car insurance NOT to be automatically renewed when the current cover expired – the intention was to shop around for a cheaper deal before renewal. On my arrival, I had to go and pick up one of my little girls from school. I noticed a police car driving behind me, no sirens, no signalling, nothing. I didn't feel I had done anything wrong and so I assumed that once I branched into my child's school compound, they would pass along – I was wrong, they entered the compound with me. Long story short, they informed me their system had detected I was driving without insurance – it had expired 2 days prior to my arrival back in London and it hadn't even crossed my mind – but that is NOT an excuse that will carry any weight with a British police officer.

So, my car was impounded, and I was forced to take out the child's bicycle, scooters and other things out of the car and return home with my child on foot – that was my lesson on keeping vehicles insured, taxed, road worthy etc. In fact, I remember that while I was standing in front of the police officers, I smiled at one point, excited about the efficient impounding process. I was thinking, if this was Africa, some underpaid policeman would have been bribed for much less. Sadly, it is true and that was a truth I had to face up to. And it didn't end there – a month after that, I got a letter from the court instructing me to pay another £250 for the offense and £315 to collect the car from the impound yard. Now, that is a lesson you don't want to repeat, and that's exactly why the system works – the cost of offending is much more than the cost of obeying the law.

The efficiency of it all is that when a British Traffic Police stops you, it is not because he is working on the probability that something will be wrong with your vehicle or the way you are driving when he or she speaks to you – it is because 90% of the time in my estimation, there was indeed something wrong, and they very likely have their evidence already lined up before stopping you. It extends to a vehicle parked in your own house – if they need to find you, they will. But surely that won't happen in many African countries because street addressing systems hardly exist except for well-built areas within cities, a situation I pray changes not only because it will help with law and order – but also commerce and urban administration.

My second experience was on the road in front of my house. I came home very late and tired on a Friday and parked my car behind a neighbour's. Woke up late the following day and walked out to drive to the gym at 3pm – my car was nowhere to be found. I thought I was in a movie or a dream. It's interesting how in London, everyone seems to simply mind their business so, not even the neighbours admitted seeing anything. I called the police only to be told the car had been towed away. I found out later the reason for the towing – one of my car tires had crossed the line markings for disabled parking. Yes, half of one tire had cost me £270 to get my car back – I have both receipts framed.

Now, would anyone want to fall foul of the law after just two such experiences? Never.

No wonder when we go back home to Africa these days *(and am sure there are many who share this feeling)*, it's easy to tell just from the way we drive – who is local and who is foreign.

Folks like us tend to be called *"soft drivers"* because we irritate the locals by trying to get everything right on the road. I am told the easiest way to spot *"foreign soft drivers"* in certain African countries is – we always strap our seatbelts on, we stop for pedestrians at Zebra and Pelican crossings, we never use our horns no matter how provoked we are and we are the easiest to cheat in heavy traffic.

Oh well, welcome to the soft drivers' club – discipline has a way of making one sober – innit?

CHAPTER 18

You Get Me Though, Innit!

When an African who has been living a while in the United States speaks – you readily understand where the slang is coming from. They just seem to have the pronunciation of their words so rounded on the edges it feels like Michael Douglas' movie – *"Romancing the Stone."* When an African from Britain goes back home to Africa, he must mention the magic word to be considered as slanging – and that word is – *"innit."*

I find it so hilarious because the truth is, *"innit"* is not even a traditional English slang – it is confined largely to the south of London and it is the slang of youth. The next time you feel no one is *"feeling"* your British slang back home in Africa, just start dropping the *"innit"*.

Well, if you are wondering what all the fuss about this word *"innit"* is – there isn't. It simply is an urban term or slang used largely in south London to mean – *"isn't it?"* or *"really?"* or *"seriously?"* or *"I know right"* or *"do you get what I mean?"* – you get the picture am sure.

If you are new in London however and had to, out of necessity interact with the youth, especially in areas of high black population, believe me the index of urban terminologies can be overwhelming. In fact, hearing them speak among themselves, you might be forgiven for thinking they were speaking a different dialect of the English language. I don't go out of my way to learn this urban slang but my past work as a youth basketball coach meant I was in their circles and spoke their language, so we connected as a team.

The first time I sat with a youth in a full-blown conversation, I confess I only understood fifty per cent of what he said – the rest, I had to figure out! After he left, I just whispered to myself – *"like seriously?"* *"How can you talk like this and expect to be a world player?"* The paradox however is, the world is becoming *"all embracing"* and it could well be that this slang will partly replace traditional English language, for urban dwellers at least – its already started in music, with *"grime and garage"* genres now very popular. Anything is possible these days you know – we are in an age of continuous disruption and it would seem the more disruptive it is, the better it is embraced. Innit though?

The term *"Bruv"* is a common one –meaning *"brother."* This one is interesting because girls use it too, so the inclination is not to see it in the light of its source word *"brother"* which means a male sibling but rather as terminology of *"fellowship,"* *"oneness"* or *"fraternity."* Interestingly *"Bruv"* has evolved over time into two words – *"blood"* which is by and large a "bruv" of the same race and *"Cuz" (cousin)* which is a *"bruv"* of a different race. Racial differentiation? Hey! I don't know, I didn't invent the terminology – personally, I always preferred to use *"bruv"* – blood just feels too "Gangster" for me.

So, innit bruv? Yeah, now we are getting the hang of it. Oh, how could I have forgotten the word *"Fam" (short for "family")* – used to address anyone who is a member of one's clique or gang or circle of friends. Yeah fam!

Frankly, most migrant Africans don't really care or even speak the slang. That's different though, for their children born here – they will pick one or two up no matter how excluded they are from the south. It's that contagious. Of course, there are many others, oh, so many others we can't even begin to count, but perhaps a few of these you will recognise:

Allow it – meaning *"stop it right there"* – usable either as a compliment to mean for example this is so deep I don't want to hear more, so just stop it right there.

Bare – meaning, *"a lot of"* – *"bruv, there was like 'bare' people at the gig"* – there was a lot of people at the event

Beast/Sick – meaning, *"amazing or fantastic"* – *"fam, my pops just got a Mercedes and it is 'sick' bruv. And the V.10 engine inside is a beast bruv"* – to wit, my dad just got a really cool Mercedes with an amazing engine.

Taking the piss/mick – meaning *"patronising"* – *"bruv, you can't tell me you don't have my money, 'cos I fink you are just taking the piss"* – to wit, telling me you don't have my money is a bit patronising don't you think?

Criss/Crisp/Mint – meaning *"sleek, sharp, on point"* – *"blood you know them jeans you bought last week, they are proper crisp"* – to wit, that's some sleek pair of jeans you got last week

Fink – meaning *"think"* – am sure you've heard that one hundreds if not thousands of time. I won't be surprised you even use it a lot without realising it!

And oh, that's the other thing about British slangs:

"th" gets substituted with an *"f"* – so, think sounds *"fink"*, thank you sounds *"fank you"*, things sound *"fings"*

Then of course there's the thing about slangers going silent on some *"Ts"* – so, water sounds like *"wa-ah"* and matter sounds like *"ma-ah"* and theatre sounds like *"fe-eh-ah"*, and out sounds like *"ah-ow,"* British sounds *"Bri-ish"*

By the way:

"Skint" means being broke;

"Heads" means people

"Jakes" means police on foot

"Militant" means being uncompromising or troublesome

"Rents" means parents

"Tourist" means an ignorant or clueless person

Anyway *fams*, there's *bare fings* I could *cha* to you *aba* Bri-ish slangs *buh* I *fink* we can leave it here, *innit*. I need to go pick up my *mint* shoes from my *rents*.

Anyway, beautiful *people*, I am sure there's *a lot* of *things* I could *chat* to you about on British slang, *but* we'll leave it here for now *alright*. I need to go pick up a pair of new *sleek* shoes from my *parents*, so see you all!

CHAPTER 19

Divided We stand, Together We Fall

I once with an Indian friend. At the time, he lived in a rented place with his sister, his sister's husband, his mother and father – yes five of them. Crowded you might say, but they had a plan. One year down the line when I was still renting, they had got together enough money to raise a deposit to buy a house in the name of his sister and her husband. Three years after that when I was STILL renting; they had their second home.

I was fascinated by the idea of *"POOLING"* resources so I approached several African friends and shared the concept with them – yes, you guessed right: the argument became *"who goes into the first house we buy and why them first?"* In hindsight, it was a waste of an entire month of my life trying to convince them that it didn't matter – that in the long term we would all be on the property ladder. Well guess what? We've all been in the UK over 15 years now and most of them are neither still not on the property ladder nor have ever been – not in the UK, not in the USA where a few of them migrated, and certainly not back in the African countries they hailed from.

The story is familiar to many of us Africans. Indians were the most common example to me, of how this communal pooling of resources for communal financial success worked. It's no coincidence that they own most of the corner shops *(Mr Patel Chains we call them)* – it's because they pool resources, and then simply repeat the winning formula over and over again. There really is no magic beyond the fact that they are always *"communal"* in their approach and that applies to everything they do – for example where others will pay for expensive nannies and childcare, my Indian colleagues will usually send their children to be looked after by other Indian families whose grandmas were in town for a visit and when their own grandmas were in town visiting, the favour is returned. It's the very same reason Indians live close to each other – very close.

The same applies to the Jews. I believe their approach largely takes the form of doing business with one another first and foremost and according to their tradition, passing businesses down family lines, hardly ever to outsiders – not forgetting, most of them operate the financial and banking sectors of the British economy whilst the Indians operate often in trading.

In recent times, a third trend has emerged of a different ethnic power in Britain – The Eastern Europeans.

This group largely have no chance of breaking into the financial sector that is largely run by Jews or the trading channels largely operated by the Asians, so what do they do? They break into the labour intensive and artisan sectors and guess what? They are succeeding. But beyond that, their ruthless ability to defer their comfort and gratification is inspiring to observe. I have personally seen a single room rented by a person and yet occupied at night by four or five grown men. To them, sleep is just temporary – the big deal is getting up and working as many hours as possible, spending as little as possible on rent, food and transport. The result? A large proportion of what they make in cash, they send back home to invest in longer-term projects. The UK, to them, is just a place to make a better income. Only a few of their *'see-the-bigger-picture'* individuals are beginning to invest in shopping chains and property in the UK.

An article in 2014 by Nicole Kenney, a USA's NAACP Economic Program Specialist said, *"currently, a dollar circulates in Asian communities for a month, in Jewish communities approximately 20 days and white communities 17 days. How long does a dollar circulate in the black community? 6 hours!!! That means that African American's annual buying power of 1.1 Trillion ends up with everybody else but themselves."* People have at various times disputed this analogy, I think it's up to us individually to make a judgment on its veracity.

So, why aren't Africans communal in the resource pooling agenda? – Surely, it makes common sense!

Surely everybody wins in the end, so what is stopping us? – I mean, there isn't any specific law or set of laws that allow other ethnic minorities to pool and not us, right?

The Jews found a niche in the banking and finance sector, The British themselves have the Engineering and property sectors, the Indians have trading and technology sectors and Eastern Europeans just recently arrived to take over the building artisan and child minding niches – is there no niche at all, naturally suitable to us Africans? Why isn't there any economically obvious sector that can be attributed to Africans in in the UK?

I wish I knew the answers or the one answer to these questions – but I don't. My job partly is to stir the same questions in your minds.

Talking to friends in casual conversation, some have suggested that we are culturally risk averse – to which I would say, if that was the case, then the communal strategies of resource pooling and success-sharing should be attractive to us because it is largely based on sharing the burden and exposure to risk – so why haven't we latched on to it?

Others have attempted the explanation – we have not fully grasped the mind-set that it is possible for individuals to succeed by succeeding as a community. In other words, we haven't quite shed the mind set of – *"if others succeed around me, it takes away from my success"* – really? Do we still think that way in this century?

So, what exactly is it then? What is it that stops us from copying social formulae others have used with tremendous success? What is it that keeps us visibly behind other ethnic minorities even in the face of equal opportunities? What is it that keeps us scattered in our success rather than impactful with a united approach?

What is it that makes us stand comfortably when divided?

CHAPTER 20

The Case of Exporting Christianity

I think it is fair to say that as at the end of 2016 when this chapter was being written, African churches in London, generally trumped the traditional Churches of England in terms of their energy, activity levels and perhaps even patronage. I wouldn't be surprised if this was the case in other parts of the UK where large communities of Africans exist. The interesting aspect of these phenomena is this – most of these churches are largely Nigerian, Ghanaian, Kenyan, and South African with a few Congolese congregations catering for the French speaking African communities.

Paradoxically, the Churches of England seem to be dying off, strangled by the huge costs of building-maintenance and slow pace of activities and liturgies that are out of sync with an increasingly vibrant, more fast-paced society. It is almost as though the African communities bring with them their own brand of Christianity. Some African Christians say Africa is now exporting Christianity to the UK and other Western countries. Well, I don't think that is entirely true. It would have been, if these churches were in the UK with the mission of converting its large non-religious population to Christianity just as English missionaries had done in Africa several hundred years back. As things stand, it appears the black churches are largely here in the UK to serve their largely ethnic congregations. Just look at the ethnic landscapes of most or all African churches in the UK – they are largely black. A few predominantly black churches are beginning to go out of their way to integrate the Caucasian population into their folds – but it's still a long way from getting to ratios that reflect the national population demographic. It simply multiplies the questions to be asked – is the Caucasian population just stubbornly atheist? Or, are predominantly black churches simply not doing enough to win over the Caucasian population?

One of the biggest questions that have plagued my mind as a Christian myself in the UK has been – how exactly did the once powerful Churches in England lose their community vibrancy and national authority? When I remember the likes of Charles and John Wesley, George Whitefield and Charles Spurgeon who rocked the Christian world, it does genuinely beg the question – what happened? Some have rationalised that over time, the church failed to recognise the fast-paced progression of the communities they served and therefore lagged in shaping up society, thus rather allowing society to shape it. Another school of thought believes although the church used to have tremendous power in traditional Britain, over time, that power shifted to the political class and the church failed to consolidate its authority in the political circles – soon, the politicians who had power to even determine how national funding was applied to churches soon starved off the churches influence by denying it financial strength. The truth is out there somewhere.

A couple of things have struck me as the difference between the Churches of England and African churches, and these might be uncomfortable to some, but this is in no way intended with malice, rather introspection, considering I am myself both African and Christian. A typical Church of England parish will likely have a two to three hour Sunday service and at best an additional mid-week service. An African church will likely have the same two core services but also very likely in any month, run other programmes that last for a day, two days, sometimes even a month. I have always tended to assess these comparatives based on results and the practicalities of living in today's world. The questions I am often inclined to ask therefore are – have the Caucasian Brits who attend just two masses at their CoE parishes turned out worse off than their African brothers and sisters who on average attend double the number of parish activities each month in their African churches? The counter argument most churches make and reasonably so, is this – it is the slowing down of church vibrancy and the regular absence of the church in the lives of its congregants that killed of the first churches spoken about earlier.

The immediate further response might be that Christianity is about building a Spiritual deposit and that is what African Churches give that others don't. The argument will clarify – the fact that the economic and social status of Africans don't improve doesn't mean they aren't benefiting from the tremendous amount of time they spend in church – because in effect, they are building up spiritual treasures in heaven. I cannot contest that – what I can ask however is that with so much time spent in church by some congregations, how much time is left to commune even on a personal level with God? I mean, it is still important to build a personal relationship with God, isn't it? How much time is available to understand how the world really works and as such, become significant in it? How much time is available to spend thinking, innovating, creating? After all we are created in the image of a God who *"creates"* are we not? So how much have Africans *"created"* for the world to benefit from? Surely, those who wield global power are those in the business of leading in the areas of thinking and innovation – both of which require time.

Could it be that the time we are employing building treasures in heaven is equally denying us opportunities to represent God more emphatically here on earth as leaders in thought and innovation? And what treasures exactly are we building in heaven? The same heaven we'll return to for eternity with streets already paved in gold? Where should the balance be drawn?

In my view, the world is increasingly becoming knowledgeable. Christian folks cannot be shielded from knowledge that is becoming part of the daily societies they live in. A time is soon coming, when churches will need to be themselves, knowledgeable enough to both dispense refined knowledge at the same speed the world dispenses its unrefined versions and deliver the word of God, in its continuing unadulterated state – in manners that are not conflicting but unifying. It will be the only way to keep the people of God both in the world and *"in the church."* The question is – do the churches see this evolution unfolding, or will the modern church be run over by the age of information, just as the last church was run down by the evolution of political power?

It is obvious the Church of England is dwindling in mainstream Christian activity – it nonetheless must be commended *(obviously with Government support)* for continuing to do well in the running of CoE schools. For now, it appears this is one of the biggest bridges that connects Church of England with her sister African church communities – a mutual Christian platform to raise the next generation. The paradox however cannot be hidden – the Church of England, which appears to be dimming in its spiritual activity seems to be the one directing the educational ship of the next generation of educated Christians, whereas the African churches that altogether appear consumed with spiritual depths of Christianity do not seem sufficiently interested in leading the charge in educating the next generation of African Christians.

Are we educating African Christians to continue in the vibrant faith that Africans have imported into the UK without the effort to marry that into their education? Or we are allowing a slowly dying, quickly diluting faith of the traditional churches of England to numb the fiery faith of tomorrows Christian children in exchange for modern education? If you think about it, they spend more time in school than church – don't they?

Where does the balance lie?

CHAPTER 21

The Curious Case of London Zoo

When I was a child, I visited the national zoo in my home country – the wretched and miserable look of the only lion in the zoo at the time, even as a child, made me so depressed that I never wanted to visit the zoo again. And I never did. Matter of fact, at the time of writing this, the capital city of my home country doesn't even have a zoo. Thinking back now as a grown man and as laughable as it may sound, I think that as a nation, we were cruel to that lion of my childhood memory and that some form of national repentance was needed, not least some form of compensation or restitution to the animal kingdom.

You may either guess the country if you had a similar experience or simply not bother to, because the same pertains in yours. Oh well, welcome to the zoo party.

Later, having kids in London, I had no choice but to put my past zoo-fears aside and make a visit. And I am sure that's the case with many others – most of us African adults in the UK won't just take a trip to the zoo for the sake of going – children are almost always the motivating factor.

I almost screamed at the entrance gate when I found out what the price per adult was, but in getting in, it becomes apparent very quickly that the animals are very well looked after. If you haven't been to London Zoo yet with the kids, I recommend it highly and if it is in summer, you get the added advantage of good sunshine and ice-creams – it's all worth it.

What did surprise me, however, was that quite a good number of the animals that I remembered roaming freely in my village back in Africa were also on display here and with a tremendous amount of information on them; that was an eye-opener for me – that I had to come to London to learn about animals that strolled the forests and backyards in my father and mother's villages. My father came from a farming village and as such animals such as monkeys, deer, vipers, adders, mambas, cobras, different wild birds and insects were commonplace. For example, as I later learned, the venom of the *"boomslang"* snake makes its victims bleed from every orifice. Cool, I thought but if these shy deadly reptiles are from Sub-Saharan Africa, why weren't they in my zoo back home and why didn't I learn about them there? Surely that would be the natural order!

When we got to the section that housed the sheep, and goats, camels, horses, donkeys and the like, I had to be very careful not to say anything. Several months earlier, an African friend had brought his kids to the zoo and in that very section whilst the kids were busy reading and learning about the different kinds of goats, he explained in the most graphic way, how some of the goats would have made a nice dish of goat soup back home in Africa. To him it was normal, we eat goats in Africa

and in fact of a much wider variety than the ones in the zoo –
but to his British born, British bred children and other mainly
Caucasian visitors at the zoo, this was horrific. I must confess,
my thoughts went beyond his; in fact, I fantasized about the
goats, deer, the rabbits, the ducks, crocodiles, the different fish
in the aquarium, and more – literally everything I had eaten
back home. Does that make me a barbarian? No, it doesn't. But
anyway, the good thing is, I took a cue from my friend's experience not to scandalise my children and judging from how they
kept screaming *"aaww daddy look, they're so cute"* – I knew they
would have been scandalised indeed if I had spilled just one
thousandth of what I was reminiscing about whilst they cooed
"Cute! Cute! Cute!"

I now see why back home in Africa, there are hardly any organisations like the UK's Royal Society for the Prevention of
Cruelty to Animals *(RSPCA)*. Who will they be campaigning
against – themselves? I would bet my next salary half of its employees will have difficulty doing their work purely out of guilt
– because they eat those animals too. I don't mean to scandalise
anyone but people eat cats and dogs back in Africa, the same
cats and dogs that pet owners in the UK I hear spend an average of £1,400 on yearly. Some tribes even have a name for a cat
that is destined for culinary fate – Joseph! Barbarians? No, we
are not – the English cannot genuinely say, they never lived in
an era that saw them eating wild beasts too. We eat beef in the
UK – it's a sacred animal in other countries, but does that make
it an act to be abhorred in the UK, NO! Quails and Geese are
not eaten in certain parts of Africa, does that make it frowned

upon in the UK – gladly not. It really is a matter of choice and a bit more.

At least in Africa, we have safaris – a much better version of zoos, albeit I agree they are more expensive to patronise than zoos and of course more difficult for daily public engagement. Very often, the lousy argument gets made that most governments struggle to feed its citizens, let alone feed and administer a whole sanctuary just for animals. I agree, a zoo may not essentially be on the top of a government's priority list, but if indeed the wholesome education of the next generation is crucial for us as a people, which it is – then there really cannot be an excuse.

The London zoo is certainly a great place to go – just make sure you leave your Afro-motivated appetite for *"bush-meat"* at home.

CHAPTER 22

Living on a Council Estate

I know folks who lived on council estates, still managed to rise above it and many more who lived on council estates that never did. The popular story is told of London's mayor Sadiq Khan who won in the 5th May 2016 Mayoral elections succeeding Boris Johnson – he was someone who came from a council estate upbringing and managed to rise above it.

To erase any ambiguity, council estates are simply a community of government social housing in Britain.

Maybe it's an environment thing, or is it? Many say we are the product of the environments we are raised in and to a large extent I think that is true. Interestingly, my own experience of living on a council estate was brief and everything short of pleasant.

I lived on the third floor of a five-floor block with my partner and our first daughter at the time. The flat above us made us dread Fridays and Saturdays – without fail, our upstairs neighbour would bring a man home from clubbing or elsewhere and there was going to be very loud sex. Looking back now, I laugh at the ridiculously awkward position it put us on the nights we had had a row and weren't talking to each other – and here was Miss *"Congeniality"* rocking the hell out of our ceiling, when we could and should have been rocking our boat too. I remember meeting the gentleman she had brought home for one of the weekends downstairs as they were getting out of his car. The following morning, my very good friend JA, came to visit me, stopped dead at the car and said *"Hey! That's Albert's (not his real name) car, that's my buddy from secondary school – he lives with his wife and kids in Bromley."* I just smiled and said to myself *"if only you knew."*

Then next door to our left, was an interracial couple. Sad story this one. Guy K, married girl B, to *"regularise"* his citizenship, ended up having a child. Girl B goes off has another baby with another man, comes back, she and K have another baby. So, K looks after his 2 kids and the father of the other kid comes in every morning to pick his daughter up for school – messy, twisted, whack. They were literally always fighting about one thing or another. Living there for 2 or so years, I have seen K's suitcases and clothes, thrown down from the third floor more than thrice. I remember on two occasions, I came back from work and witnessed his suitcases being flung down, so had to pick them upstairs for safekeeping. But here's what broke my heart totally – one day, after all the usual fights, family support classes and everything else, the children were taken away from them. Yes, gone. Taken by the state to go and live in a foster home for children. I have never forgotten that.

The last straw that cemented my decision to move out of the estate was our other neighbour, an elderly single mum, of two teenage kids, with different fathers. But being a non-judgmental person and she older, I assumed she was wiser too. So, I encouraged my partner to make friends with her – after all, we couldn't live in isolation. It was just nice to have a relationship with neighbours. That turned out to be a wrong move – a very wrong move. I noticed, after a while, that things were not quite as cordial as they used to be. I figured it was probably a clash of opinions, considering we all had different backgrounds, so I got my partner talking about it and that's when she told me, she was feeling uneasy continuing her relationship with our neighbour because the woman had recently advised her *(my partner)* *"to be careful with men – they are all the same"* but it didn't end there, oh how I wish it had. There was more to that filthy advice *"while, you are with him, make sure you've got something for yourself stashed away in case he disappoints you along the way."* Surprised? I am not – my only error was I failed to dig out what other bad seeds had been mentally sown. I ignored it to my own undoing – but that's a story for another day.

A colleague who worked with one of the Local council housing teams several years later explained to me how each council block of flats was populated with persons of the same classifications – so for example all single parent occupants were placed in a single block and likewise would young adults with no family connections, and older persons with lifestyle difficulties and the list goes on. Although it made sense to me why my block at the time was full of single parents, apart from us. Nonetheless I had no way of corroborating the *"classification"* explanation.

But people gain access to Council properties for very different reasons. I even met a man *(wish I could say here where he was from)* who used his council property as his launch pad into property investing. He still lives in his council property, drives a Mercedes, and owns five nearby freehold properties he manages from his council flat where he is squeezed in with his wife and four children. The hustle is real huh?

But let's face it – different circumstances lead different persons to council properties. Nobody has the right to judge them and those unfortunate circumstances. But it is also true at, least from my personal experience, that there are places and neighbourhoods in London and everywhere else in the UK that exponentially increase one's chances of success and a better standard of life, merely from the connections they afford. I suppose if you live in an environment where success and a high standard of living is *"normal"* it rubs off on you, it inspires you, it pushes you to do more – somehow some way, it also becomes *"normal"* to you.

Council estate rent may be very cheap or even free. It could genuinely or dubiously get one on the property ladder, even if it is a tougher option, but the downsides are tremendous especially if there are children involved. The stories of some, the depressions of others, the lost hopes, the hustle mentality, the trust issues, the wild, the rejection and so on that abound on estates – it all rubs on you. Maybe not immediately – but a seed, is a seed.

I have a friend – one, who was very helpful to me at crucial point in my life. I remember how she would always say; it was better to live in a tiny bedsit located above a shop in the best neighbourhood, than in a five-bedroom council property *(and there are council properties like that)* in the wrong neighbourhood. And I believe her. Interestingly, location, as trivial as it may appear, affects crucial things like choices of school, access to credit, and general standards of living.

Of course, these are not things one gets told very often – sadly, they are the very things that hold us back most often.

CHAPTER 23

Snow White and the African Prince

The day I first saw snow – I was angry. Not because I was cold, not because I didn't like the feel of it, no – I was angry because transportation services had literally ground to a halt and I couldn't get to work. Hey! I am African, I didn't come here to see snow – I came here to work and take back some of my gold. I was paid hourly at that time and so, the fact that I was about to lose 10 hours' worth of cash, especially with Christmas looming, when I would have been earning double rate, made the otherwise beautiful snow, an irritation. That was my first experience of snow.

Other than that, I love snow. There's something refreshing about it and I must confess I have always enjoyed it since. The first time I waded into it on an evening walk – it felt so good. For a few good minutes, it felt like *"Now I can genuinely say I travelled to Europe."* Hilarious. But the British weather is such an interesting phenomenon – a killjoy, most of the time, a faker at best. I know someone reading this is wishing I'll say something like *"the British weather takes after the Brits themselves"* – but I won't. I am British too now. Anyway, next day after all the previous day's snow had generated great winter excitement, the bloody sun came out to melt it all away! Where was it in the summer when we needed it to shine hey?

I ignored the weather warning about *"black ice"* formations and decided to take another evening walk the following evening. Actually, I lied – I didn't take another walk because I was ignoring the weather warning, I did it because I was ignorant what *"black ice"* really was. Matter of fact *(don't laugh)* when I stepped out of my house that evening, the first thing I did was look as far down the road as I could to the left and then to the right. Once I was convinced the snow I could see was still *"white"* and not *"black,"* I set out. On my way, I was pondering why the West tried to suggest that everything that looked *"black"* was bad. Then without warning, I slipped and fell heavily. I am six foot and four inches tall, so you can imagine it was more like a falling tree than a falling man. That's exactly when the heaven sent me an angel. A Caucasian passer by stretched his hand to me to pull me up – with a smile. He must have been in his early fifties and said, *"careful there fella, there's a lot of black ice on this patch."* 'Ah!' I whispered to myself *"so it wasn't about the colour of the snow then."* For what it's worth, I cut short my stroll and headed home for my dictionary. Black ice indeed! Hmm!

You can imagine the vehemence with which I said *"NO"* when a year later, a friend of mine suggested we take on the challenge of a ski holiday somewhere in Switzerland. I have an aunt who still lives in Switzerland. Perhaps if he had tempted me with Swiss chocolates, I would have given it very serious consideration – but skiing? Somehow, I think I must have done something to anger ice or snow in my previous life and karma was hell bent on paying me back for it. It just so happened that around the same time, I found myself a girlfriend – an English girl. A very traditional English girl from Oxford, who liked and enjoyed everything British – and that meant she enjoyed snow too.

She had a surprise for me as my Christmas present, she said, so when she asked me to meet up with her one winter evening at Greenwich Village, I was there as fast as I could. I had been a Postgraduate at the University of Greenwich not long ago and I absolutely loved the restaurants in the area. My excitement was this – because it was her present to me, I knew I would be allowed to choose the restaurant of my choice. I had it figured out – a Mexican restaurant I had heard so much about. Well, it turned out to be much better than that – she took me to an open-air ice rink that had been set up on the Greenwich University campus close to the Thames – to skate on ice! I know, right? Brilliant. Absolutely brilliant – me again and ice. She spent the next forty-five or more minutes trying to convince me that she would hold my hands and all would be fine. As she spoke, the only five things that kept flashing through my mind were - first, I had been floored by black-ice before –without the skates; second, I was six foot and four inches tall and she was five foot and 2 inches; third, I weighed one hundred and ten kilograms and she, about seventy; fourth, this was Greenwich my home turf, there might well be someone standing around the ice rink who would know me either as a neighbour or old school friend; and fifth, there were cameras all around us and the idea of my fall ending up on YouTube was a very real possibility. I finally did cave in – on condition we would stay in the dimly lit side of the rink where there wasn't a lot of action. I did it for her and partly because I had to be man about it. I did fall a few times and the rest, as they say, is history. Now I even boast that I have ice-skated– knowing very well that not a lot of my African brothers can make similar boasts - grin!

I am older and wiser now. I understand my capabilities and my limits, so I stick to taking lovely photos of the snow, when it falls, and paying attention to the weather reports on those days. I find it fascinating that the English love snow, maybe because it is hardly regular. Ha! Sometimes I am tempted to believe when the Meteorological service makes forecasts of snow, they do so because they *"wish"* it would snow rather than because it will – hey! That was just a pun - intentionally unintended of course.

I remember my family and I, flying back to London from a holiday in Newquay, on the coast of Cornwall. For some reason, we had to divert over the French Alps, and we looked down on a magical scene, dotted with ski resorts. The pilot announced where we were. Then, he ended his unsolicited but welcome tour by saying – *"now, you can all tell your folks back in England, you visited the French Alps"* – yeah, that's me – I have dived on black ice, ice-skated with stars and skied over the French Alps – with my eyes. I simply can't imagine anything I could not do with ice.

CHAPTER 24

Democracy, Politics and All Between.

I tend to have a lot of conversations on global politics and about politics and democracy in Africa. If you are like me, it's possible you have come across African brothers and sisters in the Diaspora and back in the motherland who are quick to compare the way we do politics or practice democracy in Africa to how it is done in the West.

Then, of course there are those who are eager to postulate that the politics and democracy that will work for Africa must be one developed for and by Africans and not one simply taken off the Western shelf. I share the concerns of both groups – the former probably travelled a bit, seen the way politics is done and democracy practiced elsewhere and although no system Western or African is without corruption, they simply desire the African form of politics to be without the ruthless corruption, killings, insults, lack of economic creativity and in some cases too, the blatant foolhardiness of those who would happily cling to power for eternity.

Besides that, this is the group who is fully aware that corruption equally runs in Western politics just as it does in African politics if not even worse, but that the difference is this – despite all the corruption, politicians in the West at least try to ensure that they create a *"system"* where things *"work."* In their view, if the garbage is collected on time, the streetlights work, the public trains and buses run on time, the teachers deliver good education to their kids in other words if the basics that make life comfortable are there, people worry less about the corruption – at least that's what I have come to find out.

The folks who argue that the way Africans practice democracy needs to be different from the off-the-shelf Western versions currently practiced, also have a point. Firstly, they don't trust the West where Africa's good is concerned. Rightly so, and to some extent, this blanket mistrust for the West makes them feel everything Western needs to be blamed for what is not working in Africa – it's that blanket mistrust that needs to be relooked at. That said, however, they do have a very relevant concern – Africa's democracy, needs to be tailored to the African – our psyche, cultural dispensations, abilities, spirituality, way of thinking, everything African. And that is where I agree with them – it is a daring statement to make but I could very easily, yet boldly say not many African countries who practice Western style democracies have taken the trouble and time, to re-engineer such lofty democratic systems to reflect *"The Africa"* they are to be practiced in – I could be wrong, but I could be right too!

The argument therefore easily extends to say, it is no wonder the constitution or other public laws in an African country are like those of a Western country, yet, things don't work in those African countries in the same manner as they do in the West: the laws are the same, their people, their culture, their psyche aren't.

The good news however is that things are changing in Africa, politics and democracy is gradually moving from ugly to beautiful – well, bits and pieces of it. In my opinion, there are three main reasons for this – first, African governments are now under stronger global scrutiny both diplomatically and socially. Gone are the days when diplomatic protocols required countries not to be interfering with the internal politics of others – that is changing fast. Second is the new closely knit social space. In the past, African leaders only had their citizens to deal with in the social-pressure space. It meant any social dissent against or condemnation of their rule was only confined to their countries – this has changed and the whole world is part of the social space that expresses dissent or condemnation. Effectively, the social weight is now too heavy for any African leader to ignore and examples abound – remember the Arab springs in Northern Africa, the pressures on South African President Jacob Zuma and on Gambia's President Yahya Jammeh? Finally, the steady return of citizens from the diaspora and the widespread availability of the internet means African citizens have their eyes open to what others are enjoying elsewhere in the world and as a result, are refusing to settle for anything less and that includes politics and the practice of democracy in their respective countries. We are learning to speak out more, engage more publicly and leverage more global support.

I reminisce the instances of British Members of Parliament re-signing from their political roles, some sacked and others faced de-selection and into forced retirement in 2009-2010 when they were implicated in the *"expenses scandals"* for over-claiming MP allowances and expenses. Africans here and in Africa were tearing their hair out asking the question *"would this ever happen in Africa?"* – suffice to say, the answer was obvious. Politicians in Africa happily walk away with stashes in the hundreds of thousands or even millions and billions, yet here were MPs of nations, considered as *"Global Leaders"* losing their political roles over a few thousand Great British Pounds Sterling. When I first heard the news, I literally shook my head and thought to myself, *"the world is not fair – these MPs would have been angels in Africa and here they are considered demons of corruption."* Of course, sarcasm is at play here – but so too is reality.

I am sure many will also remember the forced resignation of UK's Secretary of state for Defence, Liam Fox from cabinet, for an alleged *"close relationship"* with Mr Adam Werrity. The latter was found, after investigation, to have lived at some point in Liam's apartment, visited his office on several occasions and accompanied the Defence Secretary on some Business trips outside the UK. My fellow Africans, will go – *"Ah! How about our Presidents and Ministers of sensitive portfolios who even employ their family members or award them contracts without the slightest fear or shame, or travel on business trips with their girlfriends (called side-chicks in some countries)?"* I suppose, that's where the dividing line falls – the levels of corruption that go on in Western democracies (in my view), tend to be at levels of intent to maintain the superiority of the countries involved, whereas in Africa, the corruption is effectively with intent to enrich individuals in power. I may be wrong, but I may damn well also be right.

One of my favourite was the forced resignation in 2012 of UK's Andrew Mitchell from his post as Conservative Chief Whip because he used a swear word *"Pleb"* to police officers at Downing Street. *"Pleb"* is a pejorative word for someone of a lower class. I had a friend visiting London from East Africa at the time this happened and she couldn't get her head around it – to her, it was so petty compared to some of the things she had experienced government officials do and say to their subordinates and workers back in Africa and I agreed with her, but then again, I had to draw her attention to the fact that it only appeared petty because of comparison. It is wrong for any human to classify another as inferior – maybe I can't explain it properly, but the Western democracy may not be entirely right for us in Africa, but should also not be entirely dismissed – there certainly is quite a lot to learn from theirs, especially *"Enforcement to the letter of all laws and national regulations."*

CHAPTER 25

Monetised! Monetised! Monetised!

I wrote a book once in which I was suggesting ways my native country in Africa could become better. One of the suggestions I made was this – *"we could make an awful lot of money by monetizing one of our biggest industries – indiscipline."* And I meant it body, spirit and soul. There is so much indiscipline in our public services, on our streets, in our commercial operations even in our schools, that I sometimes joke if we were to monetize every act of indiscipline for $1, my country would have finished paying its debts and still have a surplus to set up a Sovereign Trust Fund.

In fairness, the idea came to me from my experience with UK society and economy – almost everything is monetized here. Call it tax, levies, fines, fees, contributions and whatever other name you can find for it – the truth is if you are in the UK, you are paying for everything you touch legitimately via taxes and paying for everything you touch illegitimately via fines, penalties and everything in-between.

In London, if your dog poo messes the public road, grass or pavements outside of your house and you don't pick it up, you can pay a fine for it – forget about the fact that you pay taxes for the local councils to keep your surroundings clean. Well, sorry, but dog poo is simply a different level of public service and it requires extra premiums. OK, stop laughing because this cannot be applied to African dog owners for various reasons. Firstly, the dogs back home don't live indoors – they live outdoors and make an occasional visit indoors. That's a big difference. Secondly, the dog may belong to Papa John, but it is the property of the whole community. In fact, all you should do is to say, the dog has incurred a fine and I can guarantee you no one will own up as the owner of the dog – not even Papa John.

Parking is monetized – both public and private bodies enjoy a great deal of income from monetizing parking spaces. In some communities, you even need to buy a permit to park in front of your own house. Apparently, the land on which your house stands is yours, but not the road in front of it – that's my interpretation I guess. Back where I come from, you don't only park on your street free of charge – you can even set up a shopping stall on the road, park as many cars and trucks on the street as you wish and best of all in some cases, steal a piece of the road by building your fence on it – it's a 50-50 chance – your wall may be pulled down or the authorities may just let it slide. But imagine if a hundred other people did the same.

There is a wondrous thing here called a *"Building Permit."* No, it's not just a permit to build a new house – that's the same even where I come from, but beyond that, you also require a building permit to make any extension to your OWN property. Yep! Monetised too. The logic makes sense to me though – it acts as a quality control measure to ensure that buildings and extensions alike are not indiscriminately undertaken and change communities, neighbourhoods and cities. I have witnessed single stories in my neighbourhoods turned into 6-storey blocks next door and others of similar heights, collapse to become 2-storey blocks. I am sure many can relate to seeing home extensions done without state permission. I am sure we would normally ask – *"What? Pay for a permit to build on my own land that has already been fenced?"* Yep, it's about the overall community and not just you.

I have practiced as a cost accountant – in layman's terms, that is someone trying to allocate, apportion or determine the right cost of products, services etc. I had a most pleasant experience once – I was due for an appointment at the Queen Elizabeth Hospital in Croydon, London and two days before the appointment I got a text that reminded me of my appointment coming due but more excitingly, the last line of the paragraph stated HOW MUCH it will cost the hospital and the government if I missed the appointment – Whoooaa! But being an accountant and a lecturer in Public Financial Management, it meant something to me beyond just a text – it meant efficiency, cost control. It meant to me the hospital could, at the end of each year, figure out where its biggest inefficiencies came from, and correct them – they couldn't have done it if every task and activity at the hospital was not, monetised. Back home, the *"usual"* reaction when you fail to turn up for your appointment would be *"the fewer the merrier. Ah! If you don't come for your own appointment, na my concern?"* (in Pidgin) – to wit, what business is it of mine if you don't show up for your own appointment? When the real question should be *"how much will it be costing us, if this appointment is not honoured?"*

I could go on and on about the very many ways in which everything is monetised, but that really is not the point I want to put across. The real learning for me has been this: if it costs you your hard-earned money to get things done and on top of that, you know too well payment of premiums will be enforced to the letter for your errors and omissions, it makes you think twice about the choices you make – because some choices will be more expensive than others, likewise others will be more enriching than others. It develops your circumspection. Similarly, if you know the cost of indiscipline far outweighs the benefits to be derived from such indiscipline, you are likely to think a little bit more about your undisciplined choices. What I like most in these, is that CHOICE is never taken away from you, no. I feel that is real *"people-power"* – as long as the choices you make, their implications and results are made very clear.

CHAPTER 26

One Heck of a Summer Sunshine

In Proverbs 27:7 the Holy Bible says, *"one who is full hates the honeycomb, but to the hungry soul, every bitter thing is sweet"* – believe you me, that is very right. If you are African, living in Africa, chances are you will see no value at all in sunlight. Why would you? It's so common back in Africa, it forms the NORMAL part of our lives, we hardly stop to appreciate the liveliness it adds to us. If, on the other hand, you have lived or still live in the United Kingdom and parts of the Western world, you know exactly what it feels like – to truly appreciate the warmth of sunshine, when one gets it, if one gets it.

Experiencing sunshine in the UK *(when we get it)* is literally equivalent to how Africans would feel if it started raining *"Gold Dust"* or, just rain! I often make the joke when I am in the UK, that if Africa was to find an ingenious way to export sunshine to some parts of the West, we could be rich and wealthy beyond measure – well, assuming we can sell off all our stock of corruption too. But truth be told, it wasn't until I arrived in the UK, that I first began to see the value, not only of the abundant sunshine back home, but of the many other things we take for granted – the good food, the family bonds and the freedoms.

In Africa, we make a lot of noise and long-term preparation for upcoming Easter, Christmas, or wedding celebrations, or most recently Valentine's Day celebrations. Well, that's how we make noise about summer in the UK. It usually kicks off with the long-term forecasts by the meteorological services. And what fascinates me most is that every year somehow; they forecast *"this year's summer is going to be the hottest, the longest, shortest, brightest... somethingest of all summers."* It's as though every summer had to have its own *"..est."* Five years into my living in the UK I concluded that half of these summer forecasts came from genuine satellite assisted predictions and the other half, from the wishes of the weathermen *(just kidding)*. That said, every summer did have an *"ish"* about it than any other summer past – now that's a fact.

Then, the next on the agenda for summer preparation are the early summer sales by some of the High-street shops. Yeah! A ritual where people line up in front of shops from dawn till late night, just shopping for summer clothes should prove to you how occasioned it is - and there you were, thinking Africa's sunshine was irritating huh? Of course, the shops make lots of money, considering most shops sell out within hours of opening. Contrary however to what people think about summer shopping in London, believe you me, an awful lot of those who do the real summer shop-sweeps are Africans who fly in just to shop and then head back home. You better believe that. And that, my friends, is the result and power of the four biggest marketing tag lines of the last five decades – *"Buy 1, get 1 free.... Buy 1, get 2nd Half Price......All reduced to 50%....... Buy 3 for the price of 2."* Everybody loves a bargain.

And then the summer arrives, it is not uncommon to have it announced by the odd rains, interjected in the middle by rains and given a vote of thanks at the end, yes you guessed it – by rains. Yes, it's possible to have a weather forecast for sunshine, only to wake up and find rain or a gloomy sky. I have never been sure whether these weather inconsistencies are just God trying to remind humanity that he still controls the weather, or just the rains trying to remind us it still exists despite our summer fantasies. So, when I read somewhere *(randomly)* that the weather is one of the top five casual conversation topics in the UK – I am not surprised!

The real KICK for me, as an African, was when I first experienced *"The Magic of Summer"* in London. It was a day in July spent on Clapham Common and another day in early August of the same year spent in Brixton. Yes, the experiences were different but believe me it gives you an idea how well summer is celebrated. My day on Clapham Common was a Saturday. The sun was out full strength and I heard there was a basketball court on the park, so I went to check it out. The guys were playing basketball on the open court alright, but that was not what grabbed my attention at all. It was the sheer number of people on the park, jostling for space. I audibly muttered to myself *"WOOW!"* – all this for sunshine? I don't think I could ever explain well enough how I felt. Everybody was out. I had to quickly remind myself that the sun didn't come out all year round on this side of the globe. Then of course there were guys, bare-chested and showing off their six-packs and muscles – as a matter of fact, I felt so out of place on the basketball court still wearing my T-shirt, but I was in no mood to exhibit my glorious two-packs.

And how could I forget the countless ladies lying on the grass in bikinis or close to nothing, sunbathing? Which brings me to my summer day in Brixton, South of London - goodness gracious me! For a moment, it felt like I was on a nude beach. People weren't walking on the streets nude – but where I came from, where we still wear three-piece-suits in forty degrees, it felt like I was seeing folks walking nude. Being a Christian, I must confess I found myself "slayed" but a different kind of slaying. First, I started reciting the verse 1 John 4:4 *".... greater is He who is in me than he who is in the world."* but the more I did so, the more the verse in Proverbs 27:20 *"Death and destruction are never satisfied, so too the EYEs of man are never satisfied"* kept applying to my circumstance.

I wasn't married at the time, so I made a mental note to myself: *"never get a hot girlfriend during the summer – you might be disappointed in winter."* For a guy who is truly *"warm-blooded"* I dare say London in summer is a real test of self-control, endurance and focus.

On a more serious note however it's interesting to note how forecasts of sunshine in any summer directly affect forecasts of economic activities and profits for some cities and companies respectively.

For me, an African living in London – summer was an opportunity, the closest I get all year round, to feel like I was back home again. For me, more so than for my fellow Brits – after all, I had tasted what it was like living in sunshine all year round. These experiences form a core reason now why I feel very strongly we are wasting billions of dollars, of opportunities to market Africa as *"the place to be"* during the Western Winters. If I had my way, a brand should sound something like this: "*Africa – Where It Is Summer All Year Round*"

CHAPTER 27

Savages and Vegetarians

It wasn't until I arrived in London that I knew there was even such a thing as a *"vegetarian."* In case you are wondering, like I did many years ago, that's a person whose diet is made up of fruits and vegetables, basically anything from plants. Or, if you'd look at it from a different angle, anyone who abstains from eating meat and meat products. I hear some vegetarian folks abstain from meat but use animal related products such as milk, cheese and the like. To be fair to myself, so I don't come across overly ignorant, the closest I came to understanding vegetarianism before arriving in London, was back in primary and secondary school when we were taught the difference between carnivores and herbivores. So, as you would imagine, for a Johnny-Just-Come like me, the first thing I pondered was – *"why don't they just call them herbivorians or something?"* Well, you can't blame me, can you?

As I would later find out, abstinence from eating flesh had many varied justifications, the most prominent of them being the passionate argument that - animals also have *"life,"* they breathe, eat, reproduce and show characteristics just like us humans and it is this "value and sentiment" that prevails on the conscience of some, to abstain from eating other animal's flesh – knowing very well they were killed, to produce meat for consumption. It could equally be a religious code or an ethical position. I respect vegetarians – it must take a lot of discipline, especially for those that did not start life as vegetarians. Some say it can even be traced to the Bible *(the story of Daniel and the three Hebrew boys)* and that it is scientifically proven that a plant diet is superior to a meat-indulgent one. I must confess I haven't yet researched that and I am not here to disprove or prove one is better than the other.

From where I came, the vegetarian idea just didn't make sense to me. I am not against it, it just didn't make sense to me, but I suppose it didn't have to. I won't lie to you, at an early point after my arrival, I even asked myself if folks were abstaining from eating meat because meat was expensive or scarce in the UK. How sad, I thought to myself. But that idea was erased once I started visiting the butcher's aisles in Sainsbury, Asda, Tesco, Morrison and all the grocery supermarkets you can name. Heck, they even had whole aisles filled with the processed and canned or bagged versions of any fresh meat you can think of. Then, of course, they had the frozen section for the same – I concluded, that there was enough meat in the UK if one wanted to eat it. That's not even counting the butcher shops at street markets. So, I suppose the whole thing about vegetarianism is settled by the ethical and religious values its practitioners place on animal life. Later, I would come to know of the existence of several animal rights advocacy groups, movements, charities et al. If there's one thing I have found very progressive in the UK, it is that everyone has the opportunity and a vehicle to channel the convictions they feel strongest about – charities exist for almost every personal conviction. If you ask me, that's priceless.

Later in my encounters, I also came across *"Pescetarianism,"* which essentially is the practice of vegetarianism with the inclusion of fish or other seafood. It was a very good friend of mine who first said she practiced this in a Facebook discussion, prompting me to check out the word for the first time. When I did, the African in me just shook my head - since when did all these my African people stop eating meat? Usually, as funny as it may sound, when I first met an African here in the UK who said they were full-blown vegetarian, my first reaction was – *"Liar! You are just trying to save money to wire back home by Western Union."* Over time, it's become more commonplace. At least it's a good thing to see that we as Africans are becoming less culturally pedantic and allowing the world we live in to shape some of our values, ethics and beliefs.

With all that said, well, I am still very African. I don't joke with my meat. I still visit the massive meat markets in Peckham Rye, the fish markets in Billingsgate and all the goat and sheep markets in Birmingham and its surroundings. I love my meat – that is also my ethic and my belief and I don't expect to be judged on it.

And talking about meat, it's one of the reasons why it's been very hard to move out of London. The city provides one of the most mind-blowing arrays of avenues through which to indulge oneself in the *"spirituality of meat consumption."* If it isn't the Nigerian, Kenyan and Ghanaian restaurants serving goat suya *(skewers)*, liver, nyamachoma, turkey tails, cow foot and almighty shaki *(tripe)* with eba, banku and ugali, then it's got to be my Jamaican brethren serving their roots in jerk pork, jerk chicken, oxtail, salt fish, curry goat, all with my favourite, rice and peas. Then, of course, there are the Turkish doner shops with lamb doner, chicken doner and shish kebabs being my favourites.

Yes, I am a bit selective when it comes to eating proper meat, so the likes of Burger King and KFC don't feature prominently on the list of places I would go to enjoy a meat feast. That said and in terms of fast foods, I love some of the very meaty varieties of pizzas from Dominos – like Meatilicious *(sounds very pimplike when you think about bootylicious, but hey)*, mighty meaty and Texas BBQ – without doubt, pizzas in America are on a different level. Talking about Americans, and I know they wouldn't want me to lump them in the same basket as the Mexicans, British, Brazilians and Argentinians when it comes to steak and ribs *(chill guys – I am not building a Trump Wall)*, but I would say their restaurants serve some of the best ribs and steaks in London and the UK. I almost always bite my fingers visiting places like Frankie & Bennys *(well, this has an Italian connection too)*, Gaucho, Buffalo, Preto, JW Steakhouse, Steak & Co, The Bull and of course Angus.

And I saved the best for last – my own British folks. Pheasants, Pork Bellies, Venison Stews, Rabbit, Hog roasts, red deer, wild pigeons you name it – if you want to eat meat like English Kings did centuries ago, then get on a train, coach or car and head as far as you can into the countryside, any countryside for that matter. I was not only blown away by the royalty of their game dishes – they tasted so good it changed my assumed notion that the Brits didn't know *"what's up"* when it came to the glorious kingdom of meat – they do, beyond your wildest dreams.

CHAPTER 28

Living with This Thing Called Technology

When I talk to most people who have not made the conscious effort to be abreast with technology, their immediate response is *"Oh you mean computers?"* – no, I don't mean computers, I mean technology. For a lot of Economic Immigrants, whether Asian or African or otherwise, many are just here to make some money, either to pay for a better life for their children, for their education or to send cash home to build a retirement home, so they can eventually return to a comfortable life after the long hustle. In that mind set, we lose sight of an opportunity to immerse ourselves in the world we live in, explore the opportunities it presents and more progressively, even explore how the positives we meet daily in the West could help us inspire solutions to problems back home in the countries we migrated from.

For me, technology is one of those assets Africans, whether as economic migrants or global citizens, can use to expand the value we pour back into Africa – we owe that to ourselves.

Technology in layman's terms is simply any created technical knowledge usable to solve practical problems. I think what many people misunderstand is that the iPhone they are so obsessed with is not itself the *"technology"* – that's the equipment. The technology is the knowledge behind it – the technical knowledge that makes the equipment functional enough to solve our practical problems with communication.

In today's world, technology has permeated every single part of our lives – from everything to do with our children's births, all the way to how we exit this world – whether in a casket or cremated and everything in-between. Several centuries ago, it was possible to separate technology from living life. As a matter of fact, centuries ago, living life was dominant and technology only supported that living process.

Today, technology is an integral part of our lives. I don't think we realise it yet but there is nothing we do now that is not influenced or supported by technology. From waking up with the help of an alarm clock on your mobile phone, through to brushing your teeth with a battery-operated tooth brush, to getting to work in a train or car, using computers and mobile phones at work all the way to going back to sleep at night wearing sleep monitors under remotely operated heaters or air conditioners – the list is endlessly all about technology. That's how much it is a part of our every breath. And at this rate, it is not hard to imagine that in a few more decades, technology would have moved from being supportive of living, through to being part of our living, to becoming the determinants of our living. And let's not for a minute think technology is only in physical equipment, it isn't. Biotechnology in my view is the next new frontier in which we humans will become the actual vehicles through which technology is manifested or transported – it is already happening in genetics and implants. Hopefully now, technology has become just a tiny bit clearer.

Not many years back, some of you will remember how cool and fashionable it was to own a boom box – those stereo players with super *"boom"* speakers, remember? I remember how fashionable it was to wear a watch! I remember my Swiss-based aunt getting us cool watches as kids back in Africa, with changeable coloured frames – I remember so well wearing them to school and I would change the colour of the frames, one colour for each school day. Gosh I was the coolest kid on the block. And I bet you remember having or at least seeing those Kodak and Konica cameras, which printed out photos as you took them? How about the exhilaration of the first time you used a dial telephone or operated a fax machine? But beyond these, I am sure you remember using other things like maps, the computer for the first time to compose a text document; I bet you remember the calendar and wall clock that used to hang on the walls in the kitchen or living room; and perhaps even the first time you visited a proper library or went into a bank to make a transaction; and how about using a Casio calculator, speaking in a microphone and recording your voice on tape? The list goes on and on and I am certain there is a lot more you could reminisce about – but do you realise that your tiny, flat, smart mobile phone is now a complete embodiment of all these various activities and engagements you enjoyed individually in the past?

That is technology and that's a trend you can expect to continue – the different components of our lives shrinking into ever-smaller operations.

In the future, we are likely to become a complete embodiment of ourselves and everything technology is to us today. In other words, I foresee a future in which instead of technology and us acting side by side as partners in the process of living life – technology will reside within us and we will become fully integrated, fully capable. I can foresee a future where things like Google search engines, and cloud databases, repositories and functional applications will, through biotechnologies, especially genetic programming, be hardwired into our humanities. We will become the full embodiments of the technologies we create and here is the scary bit – these technologies will take the lead in HOW we live life.

Today is just the beginning. Driverless cars are here, we can regulate the music in our houses remotely, turn the heating on and off, air conditioners, lights, ovens and door locks from 5,000 miles away from home. We are now face to face with artificial intelligence and technologies that allow equipment to think for itself – and for us, eventually.

I remember a very good friend of mine, RG, telling me he made a trip to London *(he is based in West Africa)*. He had to use the toilet whilst attending a meeting. After using the toilet in haste, he got up to flush away his *"organic downloads"* only to find no knobs for the job. He looked everywhere in the "little room," touched every part of the cistern – but nothing. What was supposed to be a wonderfully easing experience turned to be leading to a bout of hysteria and in all of this, the concern was not so much of not finding the flush – it was the embarrassment of being marked as the gentleman who left his *"organic download"* unflushed. Torn between his frustration and missing the rest of his meeting, he turned his back and headed for the door of the loo – then he heard the toilet flush. Now the worry grew even worse, because immediately, his theory was this – was someone watching him on camera who remotely operated the toilet flush on noticing I was walking out unflushed? Had they seen everything that happened? The mystery was only solved when later that week he departed via a London Airport and had to use the urinals – he noticed the body sensors on the walls that flushed out automatically once the user walked away from the cistern. He shook his head, laughed at himself and blurted in anguished disgust – *"malakaafa technology."*

CHAPTER 29

Football.... Football....Football

There is something about football in England. No, I am not talking about their national football team, sorry – all puns intended only if the reader believes they are intended by unintentional means that have been intentionally acted upon!

I am talking about football at club level. It is so electric it is impossible not to get drawn into it even if you are not a diehard football fan and believe me in England, there are real diehard fans. My African brothers back home only argue a lot to prove the depth of their commitment to their local clubs. I am talking about the kind of diehard fans in England who have permanent body tattoos of their club crests, mottos, club idols etc.; diehard fans who buy season tickets to attend ALL their team's games. The variant is that some will manage to attend all their team's home and away games. Some will fight just to prove a point about their teams and others have been known to die in the process. These are fans that literally put their money, their time, their lives where their mouths and hearts are and together with the media, they give football a passion and presence I have not seen elsewhere.

People claim the English Premier leagues pay players too much money for just playing football, but they forget this is not all just about football – these are all interconnected business empires. The better, the crazier, the more loved the game and the more twisted the controversies – all go to create windows into the emotions of the public and it is through those emotional windows and doors that other aspects of the marketing ecosystem works, such as the need for people to buy the magazines that feed the on-going game or player controversies, the newspapers, the clothing lines, the hotel and flights that take advantage of loyal fans travelling, the TV shows people are glued to – it's all part of an ecosystem and at the centre of it, is human emotion. The thread that connects them all is the players, their managers, and their clubs. That's why the players get the amounts of money they do.

At the time of writing this book, the African Cup of Nations 2017 is going on but you will not be surprised to know that there are more viewings of the English Premier League games than there are of the AFCON'17 games – by Africans.

I am not a diehard football fan. In fact, I'd never be in a rush to get back home to watch a game. But I love Manchester United Football Club for many reasons, the biggest of which is the fact that I heard of them first from my father and followed their escapades for a while even before I relocated to England. Most of my African brothers and sisters in the United Kingdom and back in Africa largely follow Arsenal and Chelsea football clubs. I have never quite understood why those 2 clubs have a very large African following but over time, I think it has been because they are the teams most embracing of migrant African players and as such offer themselves as teams the African populace can identify with – because of players from their respective African countries.

There have always been African football legends who played in the English Premier and other English National leagues in the likes of Liberia's King George Weah; Cameroonian Samuel Eto'o, Rigobert Song; Ivorian Didier Drogba, Yaya Toure, Ghanaian Tony Yeboah and Michael Essien; Nigeria's Kanu, Amokachi, Jay-Jay Okocha, Celestine Babayaro; South Africa's Lucas Radebe; Guinean Titi Camara and Togolese Emmanuel Adebayor. The list goes on.

These legends, together with more current younger superstars have and continue to cement Africa's stamp on the beautiful game of football in England. It won't stop here, but for now, the picture of Afro-English football is being painted most beautifully by the young talents of African footballers in the likes of Ghana's Ayew Brothers, Baba Rahman; Kwesi Appiah, Christian Atsu, Asamoah Gyan, Daniel Amartey; Senegal's Papy Djilobodji, Pape Souare, Cheikhou Kouyate, Diafra Sakho, Papiss Cisse, Idrissa Gueye; Oumar Niasse; DR Congo's Benik Afobe, Dieumerci Mbokani, Chancel Mbemba, Yannick Bolasie; Morocco's Marouane Chamakh, Nordin Amrabat, Sofiane Boufal; Ivory Coast's Max Gradel, Cheick Tiote, Wilfried Zaha, Arouna Kone, Eric Bailly, Wilfried Bony; Mali's Bakary Sako; Nigeria's Obi Mikel, Victor Moses, Odion Ighalo, Alex Iwobi; Burkina's Bertrand Traore; Cameroon's Alex Song, Allan Nyom; Algeria's Adlene Guedioura, Sofiane Feghouli, Islam

Slimani, Adlene Guedioura; South Africa's Tokelo Rantie, Steven Pienaar; Egypt's Mohamed Elneny, Ahmed Elmohamady, Ramadan Sobhi; Zimbabwe's Tendayi Darikwa, Brendan Galloway; Gambia's Modou Barrow; Kenya's Victor Wanyama; Tunisia's Wahbi Khazri; Gabon's Didier Ndong; and Togo's Emmanuel Adebayor.

Being a Manchester United fan at the time of writing this book has been a tough road to walk with my friends, both on and off social media. The "teasing" is that Manchester United has remained sixth on the premier league table after playing and winning six games and more. As of 3rd February 2017, when this chapter was written, we had in total, played twenty-three games, gotten a new coach in the ever-controversial Jose Mourinho, signed on super players Zlatan Ibrahimovic and Paul Pogba, the latter for an all-time high transfer fee of £89 million and still, we are sixth on the premier league table! You can't imagine the fun being had at our expense by the fans of other teams. You only had to see some of the posts on Facebook – pure creative sarcasm. A few samples from friends' postings on Facebook read:

'John Mahama ends his time as President of Ghana, Man United was 6th,

Yahya Jammeh ends his time as President of Gambia, Man United was 6th

Barack Obama ends his time as President of America, Man United was 6th

Even January ends as the 1ˢᵗ month of 2017, Man United is still 6ᵗʰ"

"Man United is very conSIXTHent in their games and rankings"

The English Premier League has also seen some outstanding coaches with Sir Alex Ferguson undoubtedly being possibly the best British football coach ever. Then of course, there are the likes of Arsene Wenger of Arsenal, although many Arsenal fans have worried about his focus on the business side of Arsenal, rather than its trophy winning side – I wouldn't know, I am not an Arsenal fan, ha! And English Premier league, irrespective of where its history starts from and ends, would not be complete without the mention of Jose *'the special one'* Mourinho who made a name for himself coaching Chelsea FC, took a break outside the EPL, then returned for a second stint with Chelsea and then to Manchester United FC. These three are special in their own distinctive rights – Sir Alex Ferguson, you could say has always stood for consistency, long-term view of his team and superior technical and psychological game plans; Mourinho on the other hand knows how to use the media and controversy to his advantage but he is equally a very sound technical coach. Wenger is outstanding for one thing – he is unmatched when it comes to grooming young talent. That is not to say there haven't been some very brilliant coaches in the premier league, there have and there will continue to be – I only needed to mention a few that to me, were larger than life.

I couldn't end this chapter without some of the highlights of English football for the fifteen plus years I lived here. The most exhilarating of them all, I suppose, was Leicester City Foxes winning the English Premier League in 2016. It was nothing short of a fairy tale come true. The betting houses had placed them at 5,000 – 1 to win the title when the season started and at the end of it all, even English football Legend, Gary Lineker who once played for them, described it as *"the biggest sporting shock of a lifetime."* Then of course I couldn't forget the incidence of Luis Suarez of Liverpool being banned for 10 games by the Football Association for biting Chelsea FC's Branislav Ivanovic. Then there was England' darling boy Rooney, swearing *"f***ing what?"* into the media cameras beaming a live game to the world - shocking. Not the best of memories but in 2014, Fabrice Muamba collapsed on the pitch in the game between Swansea and Tottenham, was treated on the field and taken off in an oxygen mask, later rumoured to have even gone into a temporary coma. He has recovered, thankfully, but it certainly was one of the scariest incidents of English football.

Let me end with a few of my favourite score sheets in English premier league since I came to the UK: Chelsea thrashing Wigan 8-0 in May 2010, Tottenham whipping Wigan 8-0 in 2009/10 season and of course my favourite of all is Middlesbrough defeating Manchester City 8-1 in 2008, two years after losing 7-0 to Arsenal themselves.

What can I say – may the English Premier League, live long.

CHAPTER 30

Royalties and Things

There is always going to be news about the royal family that comes up from time to time. They try to stay out of the public eye but the Monarchy is a fabric of British society on many levels and my experiences in the United Kingdom would not have been complete without reminiscing about them.

I was not in England when this happened but the news, tabloids and revelations continued well into my arrival in the UK. It obviously wasn't the nicest of all my memories but the death of Princess Diana was a global shocker – that was irrespective of whether one was in the UK or outside of it. Diana herself was a global icon and a combination of that, plus her royal status, plus the circumstances surrounding her death just made it all – the biggest deal. I suppose her death in a car crash in Paris, is one of those things that will remain shrouded in speculation and mystery-spawning conspiracy theories for a very very long time to come. My favourite of them all was this theory: that Princess Diana's love relationship with Emad El-Din Mohamed Abdel Muna'im Al-Fayed, better known as Dodi Fayed, the son of Egyptian Billionaire Mohamed Al-Fayed was a carefully calculated conspiracy by the Arab world to infiltrate the royal family. The theory has it that Diana was suspected to have been pregnant and that it would have meant her child would have had both Royal English blood and an Arab lineage too. Effectively therefore, along with Harry and William, an Arab, would have been in line for the Monarchy of the United Kingdom even if many decades later. Colourful huh? – I know.

But like we Africans say, *"there is no smoke without fire."* And for several years after her death, several analyses have tried to establish even more strongly, the assertion that Diana and Dodi's death was a carefully executed assassination and not an accident, as the media reported at the time. One of those was an article written by Marcus Lowth in Listverse.com on October 2016 pointing out a countdown of 10 inconsistencies surrounding the accident as follows (10) Diana and Dodi's car was swapped at the last minute without a backup car – which is obviously unusual for the kind of security detail Diana would have usually required, considering her status; (9) driver Henri Paul opted not to take the shortest route to Dodi's flat in Paris but the longest route which also happened to involve going through the Pont d'Alma tunnel where the crash happened. Interestingly he argues, all 17 CCTV cameras along that route were either not functioning or were turned off – hmmm!; (8) There were doubts around the driver Henri Paul being intoxicated and suggestions seem to be true after all, that he was found to have been working for both British and French intelligence (7) Apparently, Diana was threatened by high ranking British officials for leading a campaign to ban the sale and use of landmines – some of the threats read *"you know accidents can happen..."* (6) Months before her death, Diana had sent letters to her butler and solicitor stating that the royal family and her husband were planning her death and that it would be by *"a car accident"* (5) It took 37 minutes after the crash for Diana to be removed from the car even though no major damage had been done to her side of the car and another 81 minutes before the ambulance she was placed in, left the tunnel (4) after the ambulance left the tunnel, it only drove at 12 miles per hour (3) A Fiat Uno car, that caused the crash was never found despite a nation-wide search, (2) several eye-witnesses revealed seeing a bright flash of light at the entrance to the tunnel seconds before the crash (1) despite such a major occurrence happening just after midnight Paris time, the tunnel was cleaned and reopened for public use within hours, as if nothing had happened. A juicy analysis of the events surrounding Diana's mysterious death, and I suppose where the royal household is concerned, that's what it will remain – a mystery. Power buys you that.

Queen Elizabeth II's 85th birthday party and 2012 diamond jubilee celebrations were some of the biggest celebrations of that decade, thanks to the planning genius of Take That's music legend Gary Barlow who managed to organise one of the most amazing outdoor musical shows I had seen in the UK – spectacular. And trust the British when it comes to celebrating anything cultural. I must say it was well monetised too! I remember myself being overwhelmed with invitations to street parties and barbeques. It certainly was one of those celebrations that get well stored in memory.

I suppose the most heart-warming memory of all, was the wedding of the Kate Middleton and Prince William, the Duke and

Duchess of Cambridge. Did the world stand still? I think it did. If there was one thing that stood out for me – their wedding was not their wedding alone, it was more like the fulfilment of the fairy tale of many girls, and maybe even boys, worldwide – a true fairy tale. For some, it was the closest they would ever get to a fairy tale, and they didn't miss the opportunity to savour it. It certainly was the wedding of the decade, but of course it wasn't without the social and media *"bitching"* that surrounded Kate's younger sister Pippa Middleton, her butt, her dress upstaging that of Kate and the whole bla la bla. Of course, where would the excitement come from without a little seasoning of controversy huh? Subsequently, even after Pippa got engaged to investment banker James Matthews, people would find something to pick at, some going as far as calling her engagement ring a cheap bargain at £200,000 compared to the engagement rings of other celebrities. If you ask me, I feel she has been terribly and unjustifiably unlucky with the tabloids and the public, nothing more, nothing less.

And how in the name of heaven, could I have reminisced about the royal family without a mention of Princes Charles and Harry? Not that a lot can be said about Prince Charles, except that I have always admired him for always standing up for what he believes in whether it makes *"royal sense"* or not. It's a shame it doesn't appear he will ever get the chance to ascend to the throne, considering his mother, Elizabeth doesn't seem to have any plans to go anywhere anytime soon.

Prince Harry, on the other hand, the heartthrob of many girls and women and even men is simply just something more than royalty – he lives life! I suppose that is what endears him to many – he defies the *"grip of standard royal behaviour"* to enjoy life in its more ordinary ways. From being snapped playfully kissing a fellow soldier, to partying in a bra through to smoking marijuana, cheating in school, uttering racial slurs, getting naked in Las Vegas and wearing Nazi costumes – you name it. Harry simply *"lives life to the full on the edge or in the zone."* But still, it all comes with the *"celebrity pressure"* of not always being able to do what one really wants to do. I particularly felt sad for him when he had to cut short his service in the army in Afghanistan, to return home abruptly after only 10 weeks. He seemed to have been thoroughly enjoying himself as a soldier and I sincerely think a longer engagement would have made a good shaping of him. That was not to be, thanks to his secret deployment leaking out, even though a *"media-black-out"* deal was made with the UK press. It was the first time I realised that Government was in the business of making deals around what gets into the media and what doesn't. Many have said Harry takes after the free-spirited nature of his mother, but it equally is fair to say Harry is just who he is – Harry.

CHAPTER 31

The Changing Future of the World

One of the greatest benefits of my being resident in the UK for the duration I have, has been the opportunity to access information of many forms – books, articles, researches, magazines of all sorts by subscription. I fell in love with knowledge at a whole new level. But it also opened to me a window I never thought existed prior to my arrival here – the opportunity to gain some degree of insight into what the future holds.

Beyond just reading, the UK itself, with its relentless agenda to be a world leader in all spheres makes it a lens through which to best see and understand the future of the world, what is changing, what will become of the future and perhaps how to position oneself in it appropriately. Unfortunately, and without mentioning names, some countries will continue to be prey to others because they fail to learn, know and understand how the future will work and how to position themselves in it. I wouldn't call myself a futurist but nonetheless it doesn't take a futurist to realise that the world is fundamentally shifting direction and if one is to successfully live in it whether as an individual, business or country, one needs to know where it is headed.

In the next two to five decades, women are going to be continuing to take centre stage globally. It's already well and truly started. As at the time of writing, there are already 23 heads of state worldwide that are women including UK, Germany, Liberia, Brazil, Denmark, Norway and others. All you must do, is Google the top 100 most influential women in the world to see that women are in some of the most influential positions globally. Combining the influence of these pacesetters with the fact that the world is seeing more activism for women's equality. This snowball effect is causing women to begin to be confident in their own voice, resulting from widening educational exposure, so the trend can only continue to go upwards. And like any other trend, once a critical mass is reached, the speed of impact will either double, triple or even quadruple. That's a critical future no one can lose sight of.

The election of Donald Trump as the President of the United States of America, heralds another future we cannot take for granted. If his mass scale appointment of fellow billionaires does not make clear enough what the future seems to hold, then permit me to make that clear in one sentence – at some point soon or in the future, nations will be run as businesses. There is something about Donald Trump's campaign, leading to his election to the White House, something that also played out very clearly during the UKs BREXIT campaign. Elections will no more be won by putting forward the best policy arguments as Hilary Clinton found to her cost – public consent is and will be won by emotions that inspire defiance even in the subtlest ways. Change has gone beyond being the new constant – change has become the new *"normal"* and as such will happen more regularly, irrespective of whether its basis for happening is justified – in other words, DISRUPTION is now the new normal.

Technology was once a disruption and still is disrupting the status quo. But it's becoming much more acceptable now to expect the next big thing. Very soon all that will normalise and we will have to look for the next century-changing stretch of disruptions and my guess is, it will be around biotechnology.

For a long time, Biology *(human nature and spirituality)* determined the course of human history. Then enters technology, which succeeded in exponentially multiplying humanity's ability to influence, change or order its own course. We are reaching a state of plateau in which humanity and technology are becoming amalgamated to give rise to the next phase of human evolution – the use of biotechnology i.e. technology that will not function outside of the human body but inside of him.

I must say it's been a privilege for me to be in the unique position of being an African, able to see and experience the world from both western and the African lenses. I say so, because change is happening in Africa too. It may appear slow, but it is nonetheless happening. Although I cannot talk about it in much detail here, the combined increasing access to mobile technology and the Internet, as well as the spreading of education beyond levels of fifty years ago, mean that the new, largely youthful population of Africa is beginning to see Africa through a global rather than just an African lens. We are beginning to see the achievements in other parts of the world, we are beginning to see how those achievements manifest themselves without the same levels of rich natural resources that African countries have and we are beginning to question why African countries, with their disproportionately large human and natural resources, are not achieving these enviable feats. In just a matter of time *(and it is already starting)* – these questions will need to be externalised and African governments of the old order who cannot answer the youth-centric restlessness will start to lose followership and election votes. In time therefore, new leaders will begin to emerge in Africa, ones that not so much are free from the corruption plague, but who under pressure to catch up with the rest of the world, are likely to focus on building their countries as opposed to building their personal bank accounts. The world may have long been unhappy about Africa's corruption and wasted opportunities – but now, Africans are beginning to be unhappy themselves too.

There are thousands and millions of changes happening in the world today that will redefine the future of our lives, too many to squeeze into a little chapter. The essential thinking however, is to be aware that as Africans hoping to make a change to our countries and our continent, we have a responsibility to first consciously seek out, learn and understand what these changes are – only then, can we be able to determine how our efforts can best position our countries and its people in the future.

CHAPTER 32

BREXIT-BREMAIN: The War of Emotions

So, we were all here when BREXIT happened and two interesting things appealed to different sides of me about how it all unfolded – first, the intensity of the campaigns for and against the BREXIT argument and secondly, the enormous depth of ignorance it revealed in those it was going to affect most – we the people. But it also showed the maturity of politics judging from the ways MPs of the same parties were split on the argument for and against the BREXIT – throughout that period I often wondered to myself how was it possible for MPs in my home country, to argue against their party's official position and still retain their parliamentary seats? For the politics that happens where I come from – such acts would be political suicides.

The arguments were wide and varied on both sides. For example, on Immigration BREXIT argued it needed to leave the EU to be able to control immigration into the UK of EU members while the BREMAIN argued that the move to leave will bring EU entry border controls to Dover rather than in France and thus not really the control being argued for.

On trade, BREXIT's argument was that staying in the EU was forcing it to trade with EU countries rather than explore overseas markets where they felt the future business meat was. The BREMAINS argued the large part of UK exports currently standing at 44% was to neighbouring EU countries and that it offered stability and economic security. In terms of law, spearheaded by Nigel Farage, the former leader of the UKIP party – the cost of being part of the EU was exorbitant and the reward for it was a United Kingdom, whose laws were determined for it in Brussels thus compromising its sovereignty. BREMAIN tried to fight against that argument by playing the numbers game, to prove how many laws applying to the UK came from Brussels.

In my view, the decider in the BREXIT – BREMAIN tussle came down to the arguments made on the issue of jobs: The BREMAINS made a very concrete point when they indicated that there were about three million jobs linked with the UK being in the EU and that exiting would spell uncertainty for some or most of those jobs. BREXIT, on the other hand, argued that by offering corporate tax incentives, they could spark huge investments in the UK and increase jobs. But that's not what won them the BREXIT vote – what I believe won it was the combination of immigration and job argument that spiralled into an emotion-driven rather than fact-based propaganda. The propaganda that said that being in the EU meant the UK would continue to be flooded by EU immigrants. It argued – that would be bad because it would mean indigenous British citizens would be losing out on jobs to cheaper waged Europeans. It also warned that being 'in' would mean having to share UK's dwindling social benefits with a widening European population in the UK. For many, this emotion-fuelled argument was all that they needed to make up their minds – in part because of human nature's instincts to protect one's turf for one's survival and partly because it was an argument that did not require anyone accepting it, to have to justify it with hard facts – easy does it like they say. It's just the way it is – emotions always win.

For many Africans, life in the UK, jobs and immigration were already changing quite a bit before the BREXIT debate even showed up. At the time of writing, many African friends I speak to are already beginning to explore the possibilities of returning to their roots in Africa – or maybe it is just the kind of Africans I was talking to, but even I have been contemplating returning to Africa for a while now. At some stage one can't help missing family, the African warmth, the weather, the good food – it all hits you at some stage and it can hit hard. But I suppose what hits most Africans more is the *"pressure"* of living in the West, compared to the more *"relaxed"* African setting – sometimes I wonder, *"is that relaxed approach to life back home in Africa the reason our development has also been relaxed?"* – hey, don't shoot me for asking, I am just the messenger. But beyond all that, immigration in the eyes of the African had drastically changed way before BREXIT came into the picture – entry schemes that used to exist in the 80's, 90's and early 2000's had all been scrapped; it was becoming difficult for African students or even workers to pop down into the UK during their holidays, get a job quickly, make some money and go back with a good amount of cash and a fat shopping bag – that era was now gone and these days, there is no guarantee a one to three months holiday in the UK is likely to yield any holiday job either quickly or at all. It's becomes a tricky business, but people still take their chances. That said however, it's becoming equally common for Africans to simply make their money in Africa and come over to the UK for a holiday or to shop – and that warms my heart. It's not a new thing but the phenomenon seems to be expanding and knowing the tide is positively changing makes me ecstatic.

A couple of years back, the UK decided to cap entries into the UK from several countries, Nigeria being one of them. Then there was the whole hullabaloo sometime in 2015 of hundreds of our Nigerian brothers and sisters being deported. I know a few Ghanaians who were deported too, after which several Africans in the UK who were without the requisite leave to remain simply went incognito. I guess to some Ghanaians, it felt like the sins of Nigeria was being visited back on them – considering the latter deported many Ghanaians out of Nigeria in the early 1980's.

I have not experienced deportation personally and I hope I never do, but I can only imagine how dehumanising it would feel – picked up from the street, taken to a detention centre and then onto charter flights – no chance to say goodbyes, gather your clothes, your savings - simply whisked away like a criminal. In 2016, there was a twist – the UK government suddenly added Nigeria to the *"Super Priority Scheme"* allowing those who qualified and could afford it, to get a visa from £750 apiece in as early as 24hrs – of course the reasoning behind it was clear, they know a lot of Nigerians come to the UK to spend insane amounts of money and they will always be welcome – they just don't want the ones who come here to hustle.

CHAPTER 33

The People of
The United Kingdom

Like myself, I think most people simply use United Kingdom *(UK),* interchangeably with England and Britain. Even as a fresh immigrant in England, I didn't get it until some years later when I started reading in preparation for my *"Life in the UK"* test – a test one must write and pass, as part of the requirements in applying for British Citizenship. Only then, did I become aware of the clear differences. England is just one country. What we know as Great Britain is made up of England, Scotland and Wales, all countries. The United Kingdom therefore, is made up of Great Britain plus Northern Ireland. I would venture that most Africans living in England are more likely to apply the interchangeable use of the three, than those living in Wales, Scotland or Northern Ireland. I don't think I really want to stray into the whys of that – for now; however, it is just my general observation.

I was in England when the last 2011 census was conducted, something which has happened every ten years since 1801 except during the Second World War. For an exercise so huge, you can expect the *"usual"* difficulties to occur, but by and large, it was a very smooth exercise and a massive one at that. I gather the cost of it was somewhere just above £400 million and at the end of it, the count stood at 63 million, for the population of UK. Today in 2017, it is estimated to be about 64 million. One of the exciting things that struck me about the census at the time was firstly its highly ordered organisation and the spread of information gathered by the census organisers – there was data being sought on age structure, marital and civil partnerships, living arrangements, household spaces, car or van availability, qualifications and students, economic activity split between males and females, adult and household life stages, dependency, household occupancy and number of rooms, hours worked and so forth. It dawned on me then, the mindset behind the census was not merely for government policy formulation and resource allocation – it was also to help businesses build population centred commercial strategies. To me, that was the mark of a commercially minded Government.

Of course, long before the census and much longer after it, there has been and will always be talk about the multicultural diversity of the UK and rightly so – all one must do is to take a walk anywhere in central London to get a feel of the multi-cultural intensity. Interestingly however, the whole multicultural *"thing"* in my view is only really pronounced in the big cities – the out of city towns are still very largely indigenously British. To be fair, that must be the case, considering that from the last count, about 87% are white, the remaining 13% is considered *"minority"* and that includes the Indians, Chinese, Pakistanis, Mixed, Black Caribbean, Black Africans and all others. The largest component of the ethnic minority grouping is made up of Indians, Mixed, Pakistanis and black Caribbean. So, I suppose I could dare say we Africans are one of the minorities within the minority.

Something I found quite hilarious during the census was a light-hearted conversation I had with two colleagues of mine – one from West and the other from East Africa. Neither had regularised their residencies in the UK at the time and they could swear by heaven and earth, that there was a grand conspiracy by the UK government to use some of the census data to locate and deport illegal African immigrants. My every effort to assure them that there was nothing in the census questionnaire that required a disclosure of residence status other than one's ethnic orientation was simply a waste – they had convinced themselves beyond redemption. But it did get me wondering how many immigrants felt the same way, albeit it wouldn't have mattered much, considering we form a minority of the minority anyway.

I have often pondered every time I returned to Africa and someone asks me *"what are the British people like?"* It's one of those questions you really don't prepare yourself for and yet still one of those questions you eagerly jump into answering only to realise there is no standard right answer – who the British are to us in the Diaspora is always going to be coloured by the lenses of our experiences in the United Kingdom or Britain specifically. Of course, many simply say *"Brits are just like their weather – unpredictable."* Is that always the case or even true? To some extent there is some truth in that, but then again, we could equally also view it from a different angle – that Britain is a country that highly embraces *"change"* insofar as it is considered progressive. In other words, they aren't hesitant in making changes. Politically, I don't think I would argue with that, but I genuinely do not think the same applies to *"the people"* and their personalities.

In my view, what tends to lead immigrants and persons of other cultures to believe the Brits are unpredictable is this: The Brits are not the kinds to be easily swayed to the left or right. Often, they can make decisions quickly and stick with it – they may not make their positions immediately known, but they sure may have reached it early. The non-immediate disclosure of their positions often gets interpreted by people of different cultures to mean *"s/he is still on my side"* and as such, carry out actions based on that wrong assumption. The Brit will smile at you, laugh, go to bed, and even side with you on other unrelated matters – be under no illusion, it does not mean his/her mind has not been made up on issues. Subsequently when a Brit's intentions are revealed, they are interpreted as *"unpredicted, betrayals, inconsistent with actions"* and a host of other descriptions. The only thing that was truly unpredictable was the assumption to the effect that their minds were not yet made up – their minds were very made up, they just didn't say it. But hey, this is just MY experience – yours may be different. Over time when I deal with Brits, I ask everything, I assume nothing.

CHAPTER 34

Celebrations and All

I wouldn't say I am the type that is obsessed with *"having fun"* – in fact I have been advised quite often to loosen up a little. That said, however, I must confess I have on most occasions, been thoroughly excited about the opportunity to celebrate relevant holidays or activities in the UK, but even more especially, when I became a British citizen and felt the need to celebrate traditions and festivals that were indigenous to the UK as part of my self-imposed cultural immersion. Some took me longer to adjust to than others!

One of my favourite festivals is the Notting Hill Carnival *(NHC)*. History describes it as something in the form of a *"seedling"* celebration that began in 1959 although it was only in 1966 that anything with a full-blown *"carnival"* spirit came into being. Today, the NHC is a big annual event, happening around the August bank holidays every year and spearheaded by my Caribbean *"Posse."* If you haven't been to a NHC before then I strongly suggest that you try and attend the next one – you won't regret it. I know you would have heard about the very few and isolated incidents of stabbings that blight the carnival but if you don't go chasing after someone's man or woman, stealing anyone's car or weed, or simply *"stepping on anyone's toes,"* you should be alright. The carnivals themselves are largely made up of processions of music groups and masqueraders along the roads in the Notting Hill area of West London over a two-day period. If you have been to one, I'm sure you will agree that the four biggest ingredients that make up the NHC are the processions, the music, the traditional Caribbean food and of course the sheer atmosphere created by the crowd of people attending – purely exhilarating.

I always say the carnival is a good place for any man to break his virginity without having sex. Yep, the variety of body shapes, height, texture skin-colour and swagger, is enough to send any man into a *"mental ooh-aah."* I think though, that it is one of the biggest cultural celebrations in the UK that showcases aside from everything else, exciting blackness – male and female. Even the food served at NHC is sexy – jerk chicken, jerk pork, rice and peas, you name it – somehow, I and my other African friends have always been fascinated by how it would feel to attend an NHC where Jollof rice, Eba, Cassava leaves, Matoke and other traditionally popular African food are served. Maybe it would ruin it, maybe it will make it a lot more Africa inclusive, I don't know – it's just my fantasy.

I haven't yet been to the Edinburgh International Festival but have seen enough on TV and YouTube to appreciate the tremendous showcase of Scottish culture and global arts and music that it offers. Usually hosted in August every year over a three-week period, it showcases some of the world's best performers and ensembles in dance, opera, music and theatre. Seeing and hearing events like this makes me envious being African

– envious in the sense that I feel Africa as a continent has such wide and tremendously vibrant variety of music and arts that would warrant such events on scales equally global. Maybe one day when fate permits me to become president or a minister of tourism, I can make it happen. I just can't see why Africa cannot convene the whole world to Africa, it's more than justified, more than possible, more than due. Shamefully, not an awful lot of indigenous black Africans living in the UK attend events like the Edinburgh International Festival – why, I don't know. Maybe it's just not in our cultural upbringing, even although it is an opportunity for us to experience other cultures through the eyes of the arts and to see our own African arts through the lenses of global culture.

The traditional celebrations like Christmas and Easter are standard – almost every African celebrates them. Then of course, there is the Muslim Eid Ul-Fitr celebration that marks the end of a month of fasting. I am not quite sure how massive the celebration for this is in the UK but I can remember, having lived in many African countries, notably Nigeria and Ghana, Eid Ul-Fitr celebrations are huge, well the food part of it, at least. I remember our Muslim neighbours either sent over chunky portions of slaughtered cattle or invited us over to eat communally. That was always the enjoyable bit.

Then, there are the Hindu celebrations of Diwali as well as the Jewish Hanukkah. Both, representing a celebration of "Light" of some sort, and as I have found out, both traditionally involve lighting a lamp or candle.

I love Mothers' day celebrations. In the UK, it is usually the Sunday, three weeks before Easter and I think it's just sweet to be able to set a day aside to honour mothers. I remember when I witnessed the birthing of my first daughter, it had such an effect on me, that I picked up a phone, called my mother in Ghana and thanked her for giving birth to me – with my big head, it must have been hard. Some experiences stay with you. Since then, it has always been a joy to call up my mum from the UK and do the needful. The only problem with Mothers' Day for me, and I am sure for others too, is this – in most West African countries, for example, Mothers' day is celebrated based on the American diary that is, the second Sunday in May. So, after my usual *"Western-Union-supported"* Mothers' Day well wishes in March each year, my mum usually gets a call from my Canada based sister in May, also wishing her the same – the query I usually get after that is, *"how come your sister called me for the May Mothers' day festival and you didn't?"* I have since given up trying to explain that it is all one celebration that differs based on our locations. I think I have found an easier approach to simply wish her well on both Mothers' Day – who doesn't like too much of a good thing huh?

There is one UK celebration I particularly like because of its history – it's the Guy Fawkes day *(bonfire)*, celebrated in November each year and marked with exciting fireworks. History has it that Guy Fawkes, lost his father when he was eight years old. After his mother remarried, he became a Catholic and even fought in the Catholic Spanish army against Dutch Protestants. He then attempted to get support from the Spanish to overthrow the English King but got none. On his return to England with another comrade however, they both chanced on a third, Robert Catesby who was already planning to assassinate the protestant King James I. He joined in the plot. As part of the execution, they rented an underground storage trench located underneath the London Houses of Parliament where they piled up large quantities of gunpowder with which they planned to blow up the building, when King James arrived. However, someone anonymously alerted the authorities and Guy Fawkes was caught with the gunpowder on the 5th November 1605. He was executed in January the following year – talk about guns, plots and snitches, the perfect ingredients for a great movie. Sarcastically speaking, if Africa was to set a day apart to celebrate every foiled coup, I have no doubt we would have many more annual holidays combined.

On a more serious note however, it saddens me that on one of the continents that was most affected by slavery, not a single holiday exists to celebrate the end to such a dark time in Africa's history– something not to remind us of the pain, but to show that we, as a people, have it in us to overcome even the most demeaning subjugations in global history and continue to live and prosper.

CHAPTER 35

The London Olympics

It was a late Saturday afternoon in August 2012, I was with my kids in the garden of our house when KJ called me from Ghana. Straightaway after the pleasantries, I hit first *"abi I tell you" (in pidgin "I told you, didn't I?")* – KJ was silent so I knew he was gathering his thoughts to hit back, it's just in his nature not to lose any argument or debate. The last couple of days prior, he had predicted that *"no matter what, Ghana was definitely going to come back with a medal"* – those were his words, to which I responded, *"I pray so too bro."* Well as things turned out, my two hopefuls crashed out very early – Vida Anim, our 200m runner who placed 8th in the heats with a time of 23.71s and Flyweight boxer, Duke Akueteh Micah who went past the 32nd round, but got outpunched in the 16th round by Conlan the Irish. And here is how KJ bounced back – *"But Marricke, Olympics is not all about winning, its more about participating in the spirit of sportsmanship"* – classic right? I know, because I was shaking my head like an agama lizard at this point. Then of course, to make certain that he had convinced me *"beyond reasonable doubt,"* KJ proceeded to give me a bit of history of the Olympic game and then a motivational justification, to the effect that the Ghana team may not have won on this occasion but attendance has inspired them to win on the next attempt. Now my eyes were popping out. Truth be told, I had no doubts our athletes could *"naturally"* match any world class athlete in Judo, boxing, long-jump and in the tracks, BUT the even greater truth is that natural ability is just half the work done, the other half is world class training facilities, equipment and technical personnel – they hardly had access to any. For me, it goes beyond just the Olympics – it always goes back to this fundamental reality that we have the *"raw deals"* but adding value to make them *"class deals"* remains the gap.

The Olympics itself was amazing. I mean, you missed out big time if you were in the UK but made no time to visit any of the events. These are events that happen once in a long while and I think, if one lives in a country that has been lucky to host it, it offers a lifetime opportunity to build some amazing memories. Personally, from day one when I heard Britain had won the bid, I was so elated that very month, I started putting money aside as savings to enjoy at least one activity. My faith was further rewarded when a colleague of mine was lucky enough to be chosen to carry one of the Olympic touches – she brought it over to the office and oh, did I enjoy taking photos of myself with an Olympic touch? Ha! Don't blame me, it's the closest I was ever going to get to being an Olympic participant and I wasted no time taking my chance. My biggest excitement I suppose was watching the live men's basketball game between USA and Argentina that ended 109 – 83 to USA. The excitement of arriving at the O2 centre where it was being played with my friend Kev, getting our hotdogs and burgers before the game, the pre, mid and end game mascot shows, the game itself, the announcements, the live-on-screen moments, the waves, the Hi-5s, the loud buzzers, everything made it an experience worth memorizing and from what I heard from family and friends who made it to other events during the Olympics, I was certainly right about the memories being worth it all.

According to the Olympic website *"olympic.org,"* the London 2012 summer games was indeed one of the biggest and most complex to organise. 26 sports with 39 disciplines were contested. 34 Venues were used and the Olympic square, the biggest was the equivalent of 357 football pitches in size and 8.8 million tickets were available for the events. 10,500 athletes took part in the games, with over 21,000 media personnel covering and reporting via various channels to a 4 billion audience. I remember the massive recruitment drive in the UK for volunteers to man the games, from labourers to chief executives – 200,000 people eventually volunteered. As it turns out, a total of 20 million spectator journeys were made in London, including three million on the busiest day of the games. Oh, and how could I forget that approximately 14 million meals were served at the games? With these statistics, it is easy to imagine how much business and wealth was generated for the British economy beyond the £9 Billion plus, that was spent in organizing the event. Now, several years later, the Olympic village has been carefully marketed as a popular tourist attraction, while properties in the surrounding area have risen exponentially in value. But that's not all – with such investment, the UK has become a ready-made venue for major future sporting events.

The medal table seemed to reflect the world's economies up to a point– I couldn't help but notice it was as though positions on London's 2012 summer Olympics medal table were already determined by the economic, military and political weight of participating countries. I am sure the results are close to Olympic results dating back at least the last decade but it was indeed the first time it was close to my very nose. The USA swept the board with 103 medals in total, followed closely by China and Great Britain with 88 and 65 medals respectively with Russia and Germany very close behind them. The African continent was not entirely left out – Uganda, Algeria, Morocco, Cameroon, Gabon and Botswana won a medal each, Tunisia three, Egypt won four, South Africa six, Ethiopia seven and Kenya twelve.

My colleagues and I were in a pub near Greenwich on the closing day of the Olympic, our little way of celebrating, like my friend KJ would have put it *"our participation"* as a continent. But my Statistician friend Mbele saw it different – insisting there was nothing much to celebrate. To him, my whole talk about Africa being represented enough to reasonably win some medals was just a way of not facing up to the hard reality. To him and being the statistician he is, *"Africa as a continent won 38 medals."* At this point we were all holding our heads in our hands because we knew how hard hitting this was going to get. He continued; *"Africa as a continent won only thirty-eight medals in total and that's not even equivalent to one medal per African country. It means each of the individual top eight countries on the medal table, did better than Africa as an entire continent. Even more interesting is that fact that by size, all those top eight countries could very easily fit into the African*

Continent."Talk about friends who pour sand in one's jollof rice. I was the first to finish my beer and take leave of them – how do you argue with that?

But for most of us Africans, the Olympics ended on a very high note, courtesy of my *"Posse"* from Jamaica!! It wasn't just great sportsmanship from Usain Bolt and his *"brethren"* – pure classy entertainment. The sporting world erupted in the unanimous consensus that Bolt had become a legend. The Olympic website captured it best in its headline: *"LONDON 2012 - DAY 15 - BOLT CEMENTS PLACE IN HISTORY."* After successfully defending his 100 meter and 200-meter titles and winning gold in the process, Bolt and his teammates, including Blake, went on to win their 4×100 meters relay in the most spectacular showmanship. For me, it was the way I wanted the Olympics to end – a fairy-tale high.

CHAPTER 36

The Scourge of Terrorism

Do you remember where exactly you were when the New York twin-towers were hit by terrorists, using hijacked passenger planes? I do and I'm sure most people do too. These are memories that don't ever leave one's mind. I remember we were all glued to CNN all day watching the rescue operations of brave firemen and ordinary citizens in the deadly dust and debris that were all that remained of two enormous World Trade Centre buildings. The fear was real and felt and so too was the solidarity among the governments of the Western world and their resolve to deliver a measured response immediately. It was one of those days every range of emotion known to humanity comes alive and it didn't matter where in the world you were – you felt something. That was America on the 9th of September 2001, popularly now referred to as *"9-11."* Obviously, it wasn't just New York, Virginia and Pennsylvania - everyone suffered. After about 3,000 deaths and 6000+ injuries were recorded, suddenly, even those who did not know them before, became well versed with the names *"al-Qaeda,"* *"Osama bin Laden"* and of course the phrases *"war on terror"* and *"axis of evil."*

As was to be expected, security levels in the UK shot from low, through moderate, to hovering around critical because the UK was and still is America's closest international ally. If you were an African and living in the UK at the time, then chances are that even though your families back in Africa knew very well that these were two different countries, separated by an ocean, you would very likely have gotten calls to ask if you were okay and if you wanted to return home immediately. Truth is, with passenger planes being used for the attacks, the most uneasy proposition anyone could make to me at the time was for me to get on a flight for a six to seven-hour journey – no thanks!

London was to have its taste of coordinated terrorism on 7th July 2005 that became known as *"the 7-7 attacks."* And they chose their targets well – morning rush hour, London public buses and underground tubes. Within a window of just one hour between 08:49am and 09:47am, Hasib, Mohammad, Germaine and Shehzad, named as the terrorists, had sent huge fear waves throughout London and all UK. The first attack was on an Eastbound Circle Underground Line; the second, a Westbound Circle Line from Edgware travelling to Paddington; the third happened on a Southbound Piccadilly Line from Kings Cross to Russell Square. Then almost an hour after the attack on the London Underground, a bomb went off on a number 30 double-decker bus near Tavistock Square, travelling from Marble Arch, a popular shopping destination at the top of Oxford Street. When reports started coming in, the media reported there were six separate attacks on the underground alone. The police, I remember, later clarified that they were indeed only three and that the impression of six attacks was because the explosions on the trains happened while they were each in between stations. Stations on either ends of each blast heard the explosions and reported them individually, making it appear as six instead of three.

London froze, fear was rife, the London stock exchange was paralyzed as it opened for business that morning, public transport was reduced to a minimal service and the only things moving were the police, rescue services, hospitals, and especially the media. I remember the prime minister was away on a G-8 summit at the time but issued a statement of condemnation. But it was the defiant press statement of the then Mayor of London, Ken Livingston that kept the spirit of London especially and UK alive. I still remember two sections of his short press conference speech *"whatever you do, however many of us you kill, you will fail"* and the most popular of his quotes *"we are not afraid."* Several websites sprung up within hours to spread that defiant message *"we are not afraid."* In all, 56 deaths were finally confirmed and 784 injuries. Of those who died, there were, respectively, one citizen of Nigeria, Ghana, Kenya and Mauritius – all Africans. It was particularly interesting that all this happened the day after Great Britain won the bid to host the 2012 summer Olympics. The attack offered a banquet of cheap meals for conspiracy theorists to speculate that the attack was a plot to get the World Olympic Committee to rescind its Olympic hosting award to Britain – suffice to say it failed, if it was even true.

I myself remember the London incident vividly because I was scheduled for an interview that morning and my route do the interview did in fact require me to go through Kings Cross station. As fate would have it, I left home in Abbeywood, South London to get on a bus into town that morning, midway on that journey, I realised I had forgotten my ACCA certificate and thus had to travel back home before starting off the journey all over again – it is a quirk of fate that I am grateful for to this date. And I have no doubt many would have had similar near-miss experiences.

Between these dates until the time of writing this book (2017), there have been several other instances of global terrorism, such as the beheadings of the British and American Aid workers and journalists, the terrorist shootings and truck attacks in France, Bastille Day bombings in Brussels airport and metro stations, German terrorist attacks in Wurzburg, Germany by an axe man hacking passengers during a train incident, an old priest that had his throat slit in a quiet church in Normandy and the horrific daylight slaughter of British soldier Lee Rigby in Woolwich by Michael Adebolajo and Adebowale. Most recently there has been the deadly attack on parliament and Westminster Bridge. The list is endless.

Africa has not been free of terrorism attacks entirely either. I remember several terrorist attacks between 2003 and 2006 on holiday resorts in Egypt that killed many foreign holiday makers and those that happened in Kenya. It will be fair to say the longest standing presence of terrorism on the modern African timeline is Boko Haram's presence in Northern Nigeria and the kidnapping of the over 270 Chibok school girls. Boko Haram, whose aim is apparently to establish an Islamic Caliphate in

Nigeria, came into the news in 2014 when international out-cry was loudest with the #BringBackOurGirls campaign going viral. Since then, some of the girls have been rescued, some escaped, but as far as I am aware, some have died and others remain in captivity.

If there is one thing that has become very clear in the global conversation and view on terrorism, then it is this – it isn't merely a physical battle to fight, it is one of ideology. The question that follows it is *"How does one fight an ideology."*

CHAPTER 37

Money with Wings

There's a lot of money in Africa. I don't think that has ever been in dispute. I was watching a YouTube video recently of a $9.7 million cash seizure made by Nigeria's Economic and Financial Crimes Commission *(EFCC)*, at the residence of a former executive of its national oil company. I could find a million reasons why cash of that volume will be sitting, physically in someone's house – interestingly, that wasn't the only swoop made by the commission that resulted in cash seizures. There have been several. Nothing fraudulent should be justified, but at least the monies get to remain in the economies they belonged to.

As a Diasporan, I have seen refined versions of Africa's big monies make their way to the West. In some few instances, the Governments of the West have had to bow to pressure to confiscate accounts of some African politicians they have sound grounds to prove had remitted their monies into Western economies fraudulently. The truth, however is this – others and I dare say many, still fall through the cracks. Switzerland for example, with its highly secretive private banking sector is widely known to be the destination of choice for African Politicians who wish to *"stash away their future retirement nests."* That was before the likes of Panama, Cayman Islands and other highly concentrated private banking destinations started getting attractive to our politicians.

I have often pondered to myself, well, since corruption has become so accepted as the way business is done in Africa, why doesn't an African country decide to be the *"stash haven"* of the continent's corrupt politicians. At least, I would be rather content that the monies remained and were being used to do business in Africa, than in the likes of Switzerland and other tax and incognito havens.

There is however a simpler form of remittance of corrupt African money that is much more attractive to politicians and other African money players – Buy property in the West! The attraction for this is varied – firstly, these are tangible assets that can be somewhat better appreciated and which offer some psychological security from their physical presence, as opposed to owning shares in Western companies which is feared could fizzle away into thin air with liquidation or corporate collapse. Secondly, properties in places like UK, other parts of economically sound Europe and US, tend to appreciate and as such, are not mere stashes, they are investment-stashes with growth prospects. In addition to the above, some of these properties act as safe-houses in case things get messy in their home countries and they need a place to hide away until the storms blow over. For others, these properties double as deal-making or pleasure harems.

As at April 2017, the UK's highly regarded Daily mail newspaper reports that in the three years to April 2017 alone, Africans have reeled in money from their home countries to snap up over £600 Million worth of property in London alone – Nigerians, Ghanaians, Congolese, Gabonese, Cameroonians and Senegalese being the biggest spenders as reported also by the Financial times. It is estimated these big spenders dole out an average £15 - £25 million on each property purchase, or if renting, are happy to spend anything up to £15,000 a week for up to three month stays. And we are talking premium Cul-de-sac properties in the Mayfair, Belgravia and Knightsbridge communities. A good friend with whom I was discussing these statistics, stopped me in the middle of our conversation and posed *"Marricke, do you think Millionaires here in the UK will buy properties worth these same amounts in the most stable economies of Africa just to live in?"* What can I say?

I would very gladly suggest that some of these African investors are genuine business people – but I am certain many Africans will kiss their teeth and dismiss the assertion simply by asking the questions *"doing what kind of business?"* or perhaps *"how much does the average citizen earn in their respective countries?"* It's hard to say, but even harder, is the fact that it has almost become saintly to paint all African financial successes as corrupt and almost devilish to suggest any financial successes emerging out of Africa is entirely *"void of corruption."*

With the lightning speed of its development, its increasingly attractive medical infrastructures and its endearing niche of becoming the destination for work and pleasure combined – Africa's money cats are on the move to Dubai. For many, it combines a climate that closely resembles Africa's and an economic lustre that closely matches the West's – almost a perfect combo. Couple that with a government regime that is least interested in poking its nose in people's private businesses and financial sources and voila! – Dubai, it is.

CHAPTER 38

The Untold Stories of Trapped African Women

I have known Margaret - Maggie as I call her, for close to eleven years as of February 2017 – we were new recruits in an International Development Institution – she as an intern, and I was in my first proper job. I became like a big brother to her over the years. She was from East Africa, I was from West Africa but when there are not many people from your home country around, anyone African is family enough and that's the way it's always been.

I recently attended Maggie's wedding in Glasgow – she had just turned 39. It was a beautiful wedding – simple, elegant and beautiful. I had met her new husband, Dr Liwani, several times, a highly intelligent and very humble man. It was intriguing for me, flying over and sitting through the wedding – who would have thought it? Sometimes it is amazing how life plays out. Two years ago, before Maggie and her husband met, she didn't want to know or have anything to do with men. I didn't blame her – I was there, and I saw what she went through. It was a miracle she even continued speaking to me, let alone took any notice of my advice to seek psychological help to rid herself of her old pains to give her an opportunity to *"LIVE"* again. I remember her sober response as we sat at a Starbucks Café on the corner of London Bridge, so vividly – *"yeah, you're right, am not living anymore I'm just existing."* But it had not always been so.

When I first met Maggie, she was in love. She was in love with Rex. Rex had come over to the UK to study for his Doctorate in something related to occupational psychology I vaguely remember. It was obvious why Maggie got hooked – he was a charmer, but beyond that he was intelligent.

My concerns started when I found out later that Maggie was sponsoring the second half of Rex's Doctorial course and his upkeep because, Rex's sponsorship got withdrawn due to some political issues back in his home country – that is what I was told. I knew that there was a very thin line here – if I spoke up, would I be perceived as looking out for her or intruding in a grown woman's personal life? Being the auditor and forensic person that I was, I had several questions running through my head. I tested the waters, asked a few of them and then stopped. As far as Maggie was concerned, she didn't see anything the matter, she believed in Rex and besides, as she put it, *"she was helping him build their world together."* I suppose when the heart engages, it is always going to be hard to let the mind take a different path. In hindsight, I realise that the reason it didn't bother her too much was because she was making a very healthy salary. Bless her heart – she found love, and was helping a man she believed loved her back and it would have been hard to prove he didn't love her, he did everything right, oh yes, he smiled and flattered as he used her money.

For two good years, perhaps even more, she concentrated on Rex. Then the house of cards came tumbling down with just two months to the end of his study. I was in Bukavu in DR Congo when her message came through– she was crushed. Luckily, I was returning the following day. When I finally met up with her, she poured it all out to me. I had chosen we meet at the Kennington Park hoping that in that open space she would have enough room to cry if she needed to, and cry she did. I could tell she was crushed, who wouldn't be? It turned out that Rex did not actually have his PhD sponsorship terminated. No. He was still getting it all and saving it all. But there was more, much more. He had been working too, and together with his sponsorship savings, had managed to put together a 5% deposit for a one-bedroom house somewhere in Surbiton. How she came by this information I didn't want to know, at least not amid her grief. As I was calming her, she literally started to wail. I was shocked and embarrassed and I found myself scrambling around desperately for the right words to say, *"Oh God, are you OK, what's the matter, are you in pain?"* She was shaking her head vehemently. She had, by this time, given up the use of the handkerchief I offered her.

"Is there more?" I asked, half afraid she would say *"yes"* but hoping it would take us out of wailing territory. She nodded. *"Oh Jesus!"* – at this point, I simply sat and waited for her to finish her desperate crying. She tried several times to get it out, but each time, the tears almost choked her. It was about the fifth time she managed to blurt it out

"he...(gasp) he.he.. he (gasp) he is... is (gasp)... he's married ... married back home!"

I, who was supposed to be consoling her, felt the blow and a bit of what she felt – defrauded, used, and angry; very angry.

That night, and the two nights that followed, I had to call in a favour of another female friend to host Maggie until she was calmed enough not to contemplate the unthinkable. The days, the weeks, the months that followed were a real test. Thankfully, she came through it but at a price – she shut the world out. Nothing mattered anymore and I had no doubt in my mind that anyone else would have reacted very similarly.

Just before her wedding, Maggie and I met up and I reminded her of how far she had come since her experiences with Rex – she smiled, *"you know Marricke, everything I invested in Rex, was a seed sown to reap my reward, my Dr Liwani. I literally poured my life into Rex and lost everything, I gave nothing for Liwani, yet he has poured out so much more into me – a paradox of life huh?"* I smiled *"yes,"* it was good to see her so happy, very good.

Do all African women abroad go through this? No, but I can equally say Maggie's is not an isolated story either. Many have silently had to bear the pain of similar wrongs or worse and for those who have been unlucky, the damage has sometimes been irreparable. I know people whose men run off after they got pregnant and had nothing but their clothes left on their backs. It's a crazy world out there.

Each time I hear one of these horrific stories I ask myself, *"is this what people travelled thousands of miles from their home countries for?"* – or is it just a case of life not being fair?

Maggie's story and other cautionary tales have made me approach people differently these days. Now, in the back of my mind I have this this awareness – *"that there are badly damaged people walking around in our world, people so damaged that a smile, a hug, even a harmless hello, could be the trigger to turn their memories into realities of hell"*

CHAPTER 39

This Thing Called Death
(2007- 2016)

This isn't one of my favourite chapters to write but when the idea first came to me, I found myself having to face up to the fact that death is indeed, part of living - pleasant or not. I may not be able to cover all what happened between 2007 and 2016. Some were very prominent – at least from where I sat when they happened. I may not have captured the memories of those that you may have considered the most important, but do pardon me for that, I wish my eyes and heart were everywhere. So! Who passed away while I was busy being a Diasporan in UK, and when?

In 2007:

Sidney Sheldon, the author passed away. I remembered him for the book and movie *"The Other Side of Midnight."* I was a little boy in Benue state, Nigeria when my dad brought home a brand-new VHS player that had just become the newest technological *"must have"* at the time and *"The Other Side of Midnight"* was one of the first VHS movies he brought home with the new techno toy. My sister and I didn't really understand the movie much back then but the fact that we were watching it on a VHS player itself simply made the name stick for a lifetime. In the same year, the strongman Boris Yeltsin, Former Russian President, also died at age 76 – he will always be remembered for the cold war and everything else Russian. Then also came the death of Yolanda King, the eldest child of the late and larger than life Rev. Martin Luther King Jr. In her case, I suppose for most people, her death simply brought back strong memories of Martin Luther King Junior and rightly so. Ruth Graham, the wife of Rev. Billy Graham one of the most iconic figures of Christianity in America also passed on. Then finally, an opera singer dear to many hearts - Luciano Pavarotti, passed into eternity. I've listened to some of his pieces in the past and very likely will again in the future and I can say for a fact, just like Beethoven and Mozart *(OK that's a bit of a wild comparison)*, he will still be a legend in his own right for being an outstanding tenor.

In 2008:

Not a lot of sad memories in this year for me other than the death of the Black American Bernie Mac. I had watched so many of his shows and movies. Funny, he was and perhaps his was a typical cry of *"gone too soon."* For the old souls, you would remember the soul singer Isaac Hayes, passing away in 2008. I remember him because, again, one of the first movies I ever watched back in Africa was *"The Shaft"* and he sang the title song.

2009:

25th June 2009 – I could never forget that day. My idol, my musical love, my artiste extraordinaire, Michael Jackson passed on. He was arguably one of the best singer-songwriters to have ever lived – a great dancer and entertainer too. He earned the title *"The King of Pop"* in my view, quite fairly. I still remember my childhood days with my older sister watching the Thriller video repeatedly and trying to master all the dance moves. Of all the musicians I have listened to, Michael and Bob-Marley are the only ones whose albums I can remember word for word – he was simply brilliant, a one off, end of discussion. The way he died is sad, but I suppose like some things, the whole truth will never be known. He paid his due.

2010:

If you are in your mid-life series, then chances are you may have either listened to Teddy Pendergrass' *"Love TKO or Turn Off the Lights"* or you may have watched the series *"Different Strokes"* – well, I did both and so, it was a double loss to have Teddy and Gary Coleman who played Arnold in *"Different Strokes"* pass away in 2010. Back in the day, songs by Luther Vandross and Teddy were very helpful in the serenading departments of men trying to be romantic and all. As for Arnold, I would still laugh out loud today as I did as a kid if the Different Strokes series was to air all over again. He was just cute and funny.

2011:

Elizabeth Taylor, the actress who I believe racked up as many husbands as she did jewellery, passed into eternity. But she wasn't alone – in the same year, Peter Falk, the actor who played Lieutenant Columbo in the TV series *"Columbo"* also passed away – you remember the detective Columbo who always forgets and comes back to ask that last question? My father loved him to bits for the haphazard way he managed to piece his cases together. Of course, if you are British, you will remember the sad passing away of young singer and songwriter, Amy Winehouse. I hear her song *"Rehab"* ringing in my ears as I type this. Gone too soon Amy – troubled, I know, but gone far too soon. In the same year, the great Steve Jobs, died. He may be gone but he was and still is the defining author of the Apple phenomenon and everything the company and its products stand for – here was a man who represented the combination of creativity, innovation and entrepreneurship. I am not a user of Apple products, but it is fair to say, he was beyond Apple and everything *"i"* today. *"Smokin"* Joe Frazier, one of the greatest heavyweight champions of the 70's also passed – I am sure many will remember him for his clash with Muhammed Ali. And finally, strongmen Kim Jong Il, of North Korea and Colonel Muammar Gaddafi of Libya both suffered their demise, the latter, a curious case of imperialist intervention in other sovereignties – a long argument could be drawn into whether Gaddafi was good for the Libyan people or for Africa, but at least two things are clear now – first, that Gaddafi was never killed for being a threat to his own people and secondly, Libya has never been the same since that interference.

2012:

The movie *"The Bodyguard,"* the songs *"I Will Always Love You"*, *"How Will I Know?"* *"Greatest Love of All"* – yeah you remember, Whitney Houston. Memories? I am sure you have either sung along or simply listened to some of her songs lost in your own thoughts. Or maybe you also fell in love with her movie, *"The Bodyguard"* with Kevin Costner? Perhaps you were also saddened by the circumstances surrounding her death – a drug or coke overdose? I remember many of my lady friends were so up in arms with Bobby Brown for being the reason why Whitney's life got all messed up – well, well, well, I guess we don't know the whole truth, do we? I certainly don't. Robin Gibb, of the Bee Gees group left the world this same year, and so too did Neil Armstrong, the first astronaut to have ever step foot on the moon.

2013:

Many have referred to her as *"The Iron Lady"* but I have always seen her to be a woman of rare convictions. As tough as she may have been, understandably in a male-dominated environment, she had to wear the manly cloak they wore *(figuratively)* to be able to relate or maybe even gain their respect. But beyond that, it was not in emptiness, she was on a mission to change the face of British and global politics and she did that to a large extent at least in my view. She is Margaret Thatcher. 2013 also saw the death of Paul Walker, the actor who played Brian in the movie *"The Fast and the Furious."* And how could we forget the passing away of the great Madiba, Nelson Mandela. I cannot begin to write about Mandela and all he stood for even in his death. After fighting apartheid in South Africa and being imprisoned for twenty-seven years, he left prison to become president of the same country he fought for his entire life. And contrary to speculations that his freedom was going to be marred by revenge – he showed acts of forgiveness to whites in South Africa that had a huge impact and united, to some extent, an otherwise *"edgy"* nation – now that's a legacy not many leave behind. His funeral was one of those rare ceremonies that brought the world to a standstill. Around the time, I must have heard a joke in which Zimbabwe's own Robert Mugabe was quoted as saying, he wanted to be bestowed with the same magnitude of fame and love Mandela enjoyed, when he dies, to which Morgan Tsvangirai the leader of Zimbabwe's opposition party replied *"Yes, that's a good idea Mr Mugabe – maybe you can start by going to jail for twenty-seven years."* It was a year in which many greats passed away – one of them, the ever so charming President Hugo Chavez of Venezuela.

2014:

The author and accomplished poet Maya Angelou, passed this year. She still resonates as a voice that spoke for black women in America and beyond.

2015:

A personal idol, the remarkable Lee Kuan Yew, former president of Singapore died this year and if you haven't read his book *"From Third World to First"* – I highly recommend you do. It's a big book but an excellent read nonetheless. It tells of a visionary Lee, who within three decades and with his close comrades, took a small third world country with many unusual geographical and political challenges, transforming it into first world status – the Singapore we know today. He has been a huge inspiration to me and, I am sure, to many other younger Africans who believe, as I do, that it is possible for some of our

African countries to achieve these same feats in a generation.

2016:

I won't spoil it for you before you read it yourself but please do list it as one of the classic books to read in your lifetime before you depart this world. It's the book titled *"To Kill a Mockingbird."* Its author, Harper Lee, passed away in 2016 aged eighty-nine. So too, did the flamboyant musician *"Prince"* – famed *(as I remember)* for his song *"Purple Rain"* and a winner of seven Grammy awards. Quite a feat. Perhaps one of my heaviest moments in the year was the passing away of the great boxer, inspirer, icon and role model – Muhammad Ali. I well remember social media going viral with cherished quotes from the great boxer on the announcement of his death. Some of my favourites include *"I am the greatest, I said that even before I knew I was"* and *"If they can make penicillin out of mouldy bread, they can sure make something out of you."* He indeed was the greatest.

One man stood up to the United States and its allies and dared the consequences of a lifetime of economic and other sanctions – perhaps that's what he will be remember for among other things. But strongman and former Cuban president, Fidel Castro died in 2016. George Michael, the singer-songwriter died too. If he is remembered for his songs, I will happily put my bet on two of them – *"Careless Whisper"* and *"I Want Your Sex"*

CHAPTER 40

The Politics of Politics

An African politician, I was told, used to be a real thorn in the flesh of the government in power while he was in opposition – he queried, blasted, analysed and bashed virtually everything the government of the day did, said or proposed. At the next election, the same government won power and Mr Politician was still in opposition. This time round, however, the incumbent government, in a gesture to unify the national political landscape, offered Mr Politician a deputy ministerial role. The bashing stopped. A journalist later managed to interview him and one of the questions put to him was *"the government is still not getting everything right, yet, you've stopped pointing their errors out, why?"* and his response, though honest – was to me, classic: *"well, my dear, it is bad manners to be chopping (eating) and talking at the same time."* I leave the interpretation to you.

I love politics – I never used to be vocal about my views but that has changed. I have been lucky to see politics in all manner of shapes, sizes, and complexions in the various countries I have travelled to and worked in. Quite a few things intrigue me about the politics in Britain and politics as it is practiced across Africa. I do not claim to know in detail, all the politics that happen in Africa but at least I have a fair idea, having been born, been a child, been a teenager, started a career, worked and lived as an adult, in different African countries.

Contrary to what people say, there is corruption in every government system, equally in the West and Africa. I think the only reason Africa's political corruption appears more obvious is this: in the West, and this is my opinion, corruption is tempered with moderate sufficiency and very functional systems – but corruption still exists. Because of the functional systems, things still get done, citizens see their taxes translating into functional social services and into economies where they know if they put in A effort and B resources, they can get C results with some degree of certainty. The predictability and *"some"* visibly concrete evidence of things working, the laws being enforced even if selective in some cases, and the restrained lifestyles of politicians – all of these, very easily takes one's mind off the dark corruption in the background – it still exists, but at least things work.

In the case of some African countries, the opposite applies. We know how loud our politicians shout about our countries being broke, we know how much civil servants earn, yet we also see their lavish lifestyles, the big cars with V8 engines, the many houses back home and in Europe. It is inconsistent in many respects – we see for ourselves, where our African countries are economically on the global ladder and yet we also the contrary showbiz lifestyles of our politicians and the seemingly non-existent economic independence of citizens. Therefore, questions of corruption are bound to arise. If you couple this with the fact that citizens cannot see what their tax monies are being used for, the constant national borrowing, the ever-increasing taxes – then, one begins to understand the graduation of citizens from questioning the corrupt motives of politicians to the resignation *"all our politicians are the same."*

Prime Minister's Question time – is a political convention. Every Wednesday in the British House of Commons, the Prime Minister stands to answer questions from members of parliament. The first time I watched it on TV, I thought it was a one-off, then I realised it was enshrined in the constitution. I think some African countries have the same provision – but I think many more don't. To be questioning the President every week in parliament, let alone his ministers on such regular basis? *Chaaaii!* I have often asked myself, if it takes us one step closer to transparent accountability, then why don't we consider some of these practices?

I agree Africa needs to tailor her democracy to suit our *African-ness* – and that's not in dispute, but why can't some of our presidents and their ministers be more open to public scrutiny? Why do we always wait for wrongs to be perpetrated before we scream *"CORRUPTION"* – what if open question times of this nature push governments to realize *"the people have their eyes on us"* thus serving a strong preventive usefulness? What if?

I could talk about the many things that fascinate me about politics here in Britain, although I also subscribe to the reality that not all of it is useful for our African context. Frankly, I think that's one of the biggest mistakes that our freedom fighters made. In the rush to rid us of our colonial masters and to prove that we too could practice democracy, *"copy and paste"* models of democracy from the same colonial masters were adopted without stopping to ask the question *"how can we do it in a way that best suits Africa's unique needs?"* The thing that fascinates me about British politics, and to say it in a very African way is – they don't do *"stomach direction"* politics, or if they do, they are damn good at not making it obvious. Here is what I mean: in the UK parliament, it is alright sometimes for Members of Parliament *(MPs)* to disagree with their party positions and yet, those same parties will win or be retained in the constituencies represented by the dissenting MP. The reason is the clear understanding MPs have, that they are in parliament to represent their constituents, which may not always have the same voice on issues as the MP's Political Party - the parties themselves also understand that for their MPs to retain or win those seats, their MPs are required to LISTEN to their constituents. I don't know about you, but where I come from, constituency citizens are only important during election campaigns when votes are being sought – once that is over, they are largely ignored until the next election. Most of our MPs *"hardly"* vote against their political party stance on any issue brought to parliament. It's the due they pay as MPs for winning a seat on the party's ticket – they back the party by voting in its favour on all matters debated on the parliamentary floor. Effectively, MPs become the extension of the executive arm of government.

Parliamentary complexion across Africa is changing however – there are more women and youth than before going into politics. For many, it is a prayer that the restlessness of the emerging youthful representations in parliament and the inherently *"fair"* nature of their women counterparts, will begin to change entrenched political cultures.

CHAPTER 41

TV Shows and TV Woes

"*The X-Factor*" could very easily be my favourite TV show as well as, Sir Alan Sugar's *"The Apprentice."* The X-factor I particularly love, for the many sides to it – the psychological, funny, entrepreneurial, celebrity, and all else. Firstly, it showcases how a very simple show feeds off the desire of many, to escape the frustrating dilemmas of financial insecurity and irrelevance in society, to become self-sufficient and recognised – making one man, Simon Cowell, very rich in the process. Many people say its entrepreneurial genius; I think he's got a brilliance for giving people an avenue that *"attempts"* to give their dreams a shot. It's a human phenomenon not explainable in detail in just one chapter of a book – let's be brutally honest, from the hundreds of thousand people who turn up for auditions to the handful that make it to the final selection, it is obvious many will fall away – but it's the same psychology that gets people glued to their sets throughout the live shows on TV. The live shows give many, both those who attended the auditions and those who thought they were good enough but didn't go for it, an opportunity to regain or reaffirm *(as the case might be),* their self-affirmation – *"look, I could have sung that better than s/he did"* or *"its Simon's loss, not mine, that he didn't recognize my talent."* Then you get t*he occasional "Even Simon himself cannot sing"* or at the far end *"they are just jealous of my talents."* Hmmm, well. For others like me – we just LOVE the failed auditions. I mean, the cracking joy and laughter it brings me is phenomenally disease-curing, believe me. It's amazing that we all believe we are undiscovered world class talents. Watching some of the contestants that get rejected in the first round, well, even my grandpa's whistling in the shower is more melodious but hey, like they say, beauty lies in the eyes of the beholder so I guess, it's fair to say, *"melody lies in the ears of the listener."*

The X-factor is one of those shows that has broken British boundaries. The show has spawned others and there are now thousands of X-factor spin-off shows all over the world. If you are having a bad day, go to YouTube and search for "X-factor Africa" or just type X-factor and your African country, sit back and just watch. If that doesn't work, go to YouTube and search for *"Musical Talent Show in (add Country name)."* I guarantee you by the time you are through with at least 5 videos, you will have experienced the full range of all human emotions possible, especially the ones that get you screaming loudly *"WHAAAT?" or "You're joking, Right?"* – No, they are not joking pal, they are seriously trying to rise to fame and fortune. I may not remember most of the best individual moments for me since I started watching the British version of the X-factor, but I can never forget the likes and performances and pretty much everything the surrounded contestants like Susan Boyle, who blew the world away, Sam Bailey, who went on to win the X-factor in 2013 now, she is what you call a *"voice."* Then, I am sure many will also remember the likes of Josh Daniel who sang

Labyrinth's hit, *"Jealous,"* reducing Simon Cowell to tears – yep, totally unheard of. And finally, we will all without a doubt remember Alexandra Burke, Leona Lewis, 1-Direction, JLS, Olly Murs and for my fellow Africans, by all means - Gamu Nhengu from Zimbabwe, Anelisa Lamola from South Africa and the Ghanaian Duo of Reggie and Bollie – who, although, did not win the X-factor, certainly turned the heat up on it for the short while they were there.

And finally, finally, finally – if there was anything that made X-factor what it is, I would bet it is the varied personalities of its judges. I cannot tell, whether a psychologist was employed in selecting them but I will most assuredly say, their varied personalities, makes the millions who watch it, hooked – everyone has a judge they find an emotional connection to and that's the trick. If yours wasn't *"the hard-man,"* Simon Cowell, then perhaps it was *"baby-tears"* Cheryl Cole or even the *"quirky-cutie"* Louis Walsh. Of course, we have had our bites of *"wild-fire"* Sharon Osborne, *"naughty-cat"* Nicole Scherzinger and a presenter we have all come to love, *"Mr Steady"* - Dermot O'Leary.

To be fair, I am not a huge TV fan, but I have also made time to enjoy shows like Sir Alan Sugar's *"The Apprentice"* – again, one of those shows, that have gained some traction and spread. Not a lot of entrepreneurs will go down this route but the fame that comes with media expositions and associating with Sir Alan Sugar appears to be the motivating drive for participants. The *"ruthlessness"* shown by some candidates on the show constantly remind me of Act III, Scene I, of Shakespeare's Julius Caesar, being stabbed by Brutus his friend and his fellow conspirators

– just like the plight of team leaders on the Apprentice shows.

Then of course there are the other reality shows, drama series, soap operas, movie series. Whether you have been a TV
junkie or an alien to British TV shows, one thing is for certain,
you would have heard of at least a couple of some of Britain's
most popular TV shows like Britain's Got Talent, Celebrity Big
Brother House, I am a Celebrity –Get me out of here, Coro-
nation street, Dragons' Den, The Game of Thrones, Sherlock
Holmes, Doctor Who, Downtown Abbey, Midsomer Murders,
Skins, The Grand Tour, Grand Designs *(one of my favourites)*, Location, Shameless, Doc Martin, Essex, Strike Back, Top Gear,
Have I got news for you, Mr Selfridge, Not Going Out, Take
Me Out, East Enders, Casualty, The Hollow Crown, Mi-5, Hol-
lyoaks, Emmerdale, British Bake Off, The Graham Norton
Show, Taggart, Little Britain, wire in the Blood.

I can almost hear someone with fond memories of the United Kingdom, screaming in their *head "how can you remember these
shows and leave out ......?"* Well, at least I got you reminiscing and
that also counts. Ha! If like me, you've been a parent at some
point in the UK, you MUST as a matter of parental necessity,
have heard of shows like Peppa Pig, Bob the Builder, Balamore,
Justin's House, Jake and the Neverland pirates, Dora the explor-
er, Rasta Mouse, Teletubbies, The Octanauts, Blue Peter, Fire-
man Sam, Postman Pat, Charlie and Lola, In the Night Garden.
When I started having kids, I remember I would sit at my desk
at work, unconsciously humming cartoon theme songs – it took
my Director, during an annual review process to ask me *"I don't
think you do, but do you realize you've been humming cartoon songs at your*

desk?" – only then, did it dawn on me why I had been getting *"curious smiles"* from work colleagues. That's what happens when you watch too many *"age inappropriate"* shows on TV.

CHAPTER 42

The Untold Stories of Trapped African Men

"*Several months later, thousands of pounds in legal fees later, many court attendances later, several stressful moments later, countless days of lost appetites and sleepless nights later, distorted emotions later – and I am still yet to see my three wonderful children, children I loved and cared for, children I was so intensely connected to, children I would do anything for, taken away from me and backed by the laws of the land - I miss them terribly.*"

This is the eighth time I have attempted to write this chapter, I deleted the last seven because of the memories it brings me when I remember Bami's story. Bami used to be my work colleague. The sad truth is – Bami is not alone on this painful journey. There are countless African men facing agonising entrapments of various kinds in the United Kingdom and elsewhere – for some reason, people don't talk about these things. I am unsure whether men feel they will be weaklings or because they fear being seen as *"outplayed, outsmarted, out-conned."* One thing I know, it can never be a good experience.

2013 was the first time I heard of anything of this nature. Bami and I used to work as Security guards when I first came to the

UK, then we split ways and I ended up back in mainstream accounting. Several years later I was driving through town and chanced on a Bami, whom, incidentally I almost hit with my car. He had been walking across the road, oblivious to his sur- rounding, deep in thought – I didn't recognise him at first until I parked nearby and hurried to the man. It was Bami but it was obvious there was something terrible troubling him so I gave him a hug and skipped the whole *"it's been ages, how have you been?"* pleasantries. I pulled him into a nearby cafe and after fifteen or so minutes of silence, he gave a deep sigh and began narrating his story to me. In short, he lived with his partner, and between them they had two children and one other of his partner.

Bami told me after they had been together for two years, they got engaged and immediately agreed to start putting up a family house back in Africa *(country withheld)* as a financial *"fall-back"* to either rent out while they were in the UK or live in, should they decide to return. Bami was a ferocious worker, he always has been and for the last three years, he had simply worked and worked, bringing in the money needed to finish their project. He had agreed with his missus, since she still had family back home, to oversee managing the project *(neither of Bami's parents were alive and he was the only child)*. He saw the updates on the building via photos that his partner regularly received from her folks back home. Everybody was happy.

One day however, something happened. Bami took ill, so he stayed home for the day with the children. The mailman de- livered the post, one of which was a cylindrical. Bami popped into the kitchen and when he returned to the living room, his two-year-old son had unwrapped the package. Naturally, now that it was unwrapped, he peeked – it was the building plans for their house. First, he was elated, then he realised the building plans were done and registered in the name of his partner, not in their joint names as they had originally agreed. Secondly, there was a note attached to the drawing plans that said, *"You are almost there my daughter, I am so proud of you. Now our family can also live with some dignity."*

Bami's emotions quickly raced from anger to disappointment, to disgust and all the way back to anger. When his partner came back and he confronted her about everything she didn't deny anything, she didn't agree either, but she did warn him not to do anything or else she would call the police. Bami, confused, kept pressing for the truth, the next thing he knew, he heard sirens outside his door, police barged in, his partner came down in tears, he was charged for common assault as had been reported by his partner and *"pooof"* – he was whisked away to the police station.

He paused *"up till today, the whole thing has felt like a movie being played to me."* According to him, the weeks that followed were unbearable. His partner had made complaints against him for constant abuse, physically, emotionally and sexually. Next stop another police arrest and court hearing – He came back some days later and his partner had deserted their home with their children. At the time I met him, he had been served an order by the court prohibiting him from making any contact with his children and wife, here is the bit that *"killed"* him – his now ex, had reported how threatened she was and within a matter of days, she had been settled in a two-bedroom Local authority house.

This is not an imaginary story. Bami is now back in his home country doing well, and now has access to his children – but he lost everything and had to start all over again.

I will not be naive to say Bami's story was a hundred per cent accurate but I can also say it was not the first, second, third or fourth time I had come across similar occurrences. And sadly, there are motivating factors for this seemingly rising incident – firstly, it would appear, getting on the property ladder by whatever means, is one of the surest ways to financial independence in the UK. It isn't the only way, but property is certainly a sure element in the portfolio for a greater majority of persons achieving financial freedom and as such, using the social care system to get on free social housing which sometimes offers the tenant an option to buy in the long run at cheap prices can easily become motivating. Secondly, the laws are such that men from the word *'go'* have an uphill task, having to first prove their innocence on even the most minor charge made against them by a women or children, before even advancing to the next stage of *'defending'* themselves. Usually, by the time an entire legal cycle is complete the losses can be tremendous. Lastly and the biggest jackpot for some, is the working of the British social and housing benefit system. It has its complications, checks and balances and all the rest but essentially – the state through its local authorities, have an obligation to *"house its vulnerable"* in situations of need, distress, etc. Sadly, and very sadly I must say, some *(and I do stress 'some')* have come to understand the surest way to convincingly show proof of vulnerability, need and threat is through a combined claim of *"a potentially harmful man"* and custody of *"vulnerable under-aged children."*

I must confess, one of the biggest shocks to me, in these rather wickedly corrupt acts, is the fact that some of the cases are carefully choreographed acts between men and women to cheat the system – how sad. I like many others, have often asked the troubling question – two questions in fact – first, *"who in their right minds would go through all of this, to gain freebies from the state by tearing their family apart?"* And secondly this – *"are men being used as means to an end?"*

A lot of things don't add up for me, but I can accept that. What I find hard to accept is – why is this happening more and more in our African communities? What is going on?

No, these are not just stories.

CHAPTER 43

The Language of a Queen, the Tongue of an African Prince

When it first happened to me, I didn't like it one bit. Before coming over to the UK, I had received many compliments on how good my spoken English was. In fact, one of my very first managers at work in London, once described my English at an annual review meeting as *"flowery."* I partly owe my decision to start writing to him. But what I experienced, when I did, was very embarrassing although I suppose it could and does happen to anyone, even the indigenous Brits. The reason it felt so embarrassing to me was because a six-year old pointed my mistake out to me. Today, I laugh whenever the memory comes to mind.

I was visiting a Nigerian friend and his family, down in Plumstead in South East London. During the pleasantries, I mentioned I was late because I had stopped over at *"Woolwich,"* the town just before Plumstead. His kids broke out in hysterical laughter. First I thought it was something on the cartoon network they were watching. Then, it felt like everybody else got the joke except me. I was later to discover, that the joke was – me! My mistake was classic – I had pronounced Woolwich as *"Wool-Witch"* when in fact the middle *"W"* is silent. The correct pronunciation is *"Woo-leech"*. My friend reassured me that it was not only a joke on me, it was a family joke – he had committed the same faux pas, with the same word, when he first came into the United Kingdom.

A year or so later, I was to take out my vengeful humour on an old friend who had come over to visit from Ghana. We scheduled to meet for dinner in Surrey Quays at a Ben & Jerry's restaurant. I called him to find out if he was going to be able to find his way to the place – that's when he dropped the bomb – *"Suu-ree-Ku-Ace"* he pronounced it – I literally had to pull my car over to a curb, laugh my heart out, then call him back once I regained my sanity. His gaff was a classic– Surrey Quays is rather pronounced *"Suh-Ree-Kees."* It could happen to any of us. I am sure, even those laughing out there, have had your own experiences.

You think you've mastered these obscure words, then one comes along to remind you the English Language does have more than fifty shades of grey. In my case, it happened when I moved into the International Development Sector. I had had many email communications with a client from Ireland and now finally we were scheduled to meet face to face. I had rehearsed her name several times the night before. The meeting was live, and I instantly blew it when I boldly and very cockily blurted out what I was confident was the right pronunciation of her name – *"See-ob-Han."* I even pronounced it very fast, to make it sound like it came to me naturally. Oooh bless her - she giggled and corrected my pronunciation as *"She-vorn."* My face went limp. *"It's happened again, Oh dear Christ."* I swallowed hard. And guess how her name is spelt – S-I-O-B-H-A-N *(Siobhan)* – yep! And it's pronounced *"She-vorn."* No wonder I blew it.

Sometimes, I see a word or name and I just give up. I have called friends back home who in conversation have asked me if I liked the football club *"Leicester City"* when they first won the English premiership cup. Their mistake was that instead of the correct *"Les-tah,"* they pronounced it phonetically *"Leh-ses-tah."* My rule of thumb has become *"what you see, is not always how it should sound"* and that has helped tremendously or *"if in doubt, just ask."* I know why many won't ask. I am sure it's the feeling others might be thinking *"why can't you pronounce such a simple word?"* That's just our fear and a bit of pride playing on our minds because as I found out, most people are very happy to help you get it right.

There are many others. A few of my favourites are Worcester-shire, which many first timers pronounce as *"Woo-ses-tah-sheer"* but is correctly is pronounced *"Woos-teh-sher".* Or take for example, the town of Godmanchester in Cambridge, which many look at and say to themselves, Ah! I know *"God"* and I also know *"Manchester United FC,"* so surely, this town in Cambridge can only be pronounced as *"God-Man-ches-tah"* right? Well, wrong – it is actually pronounced *"Gum-stah."* And here is one I hear a lot among my fellow African folks who are in London on visit because it is right at the centre of the London high street shopping district – its Marylebone. I mean, what could be so hard about putting sister Mary's name and *"Bone"* together. So, I hear many say *"Mary-lee-bone"* – errr, it's *"Mah-lee-bone"*

I am sure there are many more of these counterintuitive pronunciations in the USA and other parts of Europe. I remember on my first trip to US, I was corrected and told that Arkansas is not pronounced as *"Ah-kan-zas"* but rather *"Arh-ken-sor"* – I was like HUH? And there is Gloucester and Greenwich, both towns in England and USA and their correct pronunciations, *"Glos-tah"* and *"Gren ich"* respectively. If you got the latter wrong, don't worry – I also used to say *"Green-witch"* – but can you blame me? I am African, I must have heard the word *"Witch"* so many times that anything remotely close to its pronunciation automatically prompted my mind to scream *"WITCH"*

Here are ten names of places and persons, some of which I am certain you have come across and gotten wrong pronouncing – c'mon, be honest: Grosvenor *(Grov-nah)*, Bicester *(Bis-tah)*, Edinburgh *(Edin-bruh)*, Guildford *(Gil-ford)*, Loughborough *(Lah-bruh)*, Woolfardisworthy *(wool-zree)*, Joaquin *(wah-keen)*, Sean *(sh-un)*, Isla *(eye-lah)*, Phoebe *(Fee-bee)*

Being African, I know for a fact there are certain tribes who do not naturally pronounce certain letters of the English alphabets. For example, some replace *"K"* with a *"Ch"* some totally omit *"T or G"* and for some, *"L and R"* are interchanged in pronunciation. You can imagine these natural phonetic limitations having to exist side by side with some of the counterintuitive nature of words, alien to our tongues as indigenous Africans. A colleague with a natural, *"G and T"* omission phenomenon used to have a fit when she had to pronounce the country *Kyrgyzstan* – she froze every single time. It took a while for my Caucasian colleagues at work to figure the problem out.

What can I say? It's one thing to claim English language is our mother tongue because we speak it, it's another thing to claim it is one's mother tongue because you are born into it – the two are never the same. Fair to say from these experiences and many others not here mentioned, I have never referred to English language as my mother tongue. It is simply one of my cousin-tongues – after all, my *"mother's tongue"* would never subject me to such linguistic torture.

CHAPTER 44

The Diasporan Wahala

It's only a matter of time – almost everyone in the Diaspora comes to that point. It's the point you start thinking, *"what am I doing here still living in this cold?"* Although most people won't voice it, it's a silent conversation people in the Diaspora usually have with themselves. Soon after that, follows another mental battle to either defeat the thought and justify staying in the West or embrace the reasons why one must return to their motherland. Interestingly, whichever path your mind chooses to fight for, a lot of arguments can be made to justify. So effectively, every decision can be a winning one. But that isn't the real fear, is it? No, the real fear is what happens after that decision is made? If the decision is to remain here in the West, then mostly the fear comes from the feeling of guilt that you have abandoned your roots for a foreign land. That decision is a lot more reasonable to make if one has secured a full right to live in the West and has a very successful career or business. The other choice, to return home for good, is fraught with its own demons – what if things don't work out back home, as I hope they will? As a friend once confided, *"these mental bouts are nothing short of Guantanamo torture sessions."*

Over the years, I have had friends who have gotten up in the middle of the night, packed their bags then called me from Heathrow or J.F. Kennedy airport and told me, *"hey big bro, Chale, this is it for me man – I dey go home."* Others have even gone home only to return to the West with the usual excuse - *"Hmm, home is different and tough meehn."* If you ask me, I think there are just adjustment difficulties. If you have lived in the West for five or more years, believe me it takes quite some adjustment to return to Africa without arguing with everyone including your own parents. One tends to forget that there is a way things are done in the West and there is a way things are done in Africa – it's called cultural differences.

A wonderful friend of mine returned home and got so frustrated setting up his company, he almost ended up in jail in Eastern Africa – in just one day! His frustration came from three different building artisans and on each occasion, the anger was fuelled by each artisan doing things differently from how he had been instructed and on every one of those occasions when questioned, their responses were the same – *"yes, but this is how we do it HERE."* They are right – there is a certain way certain things are done in certain places and having a different viewpoint doesn't always mean one is right, neither does being frustrated to death get one heard. Welcome back.

Very few people travel to the West with the intention of never returning home. I may be wrong, but talking to a lot of people over the years, it would appear most come over here with two main agendas - *"I am just here to go to school, gain some experience and go back home"* or with others *"I am here to seek greener pastures, save some money, set up a business or put up a house back home and or get a piece of land and then, I will be going back."*

Many start off with the same addendum – *"and then I will go back."* Then the years came and go, somewhere along the line people get trapped in different ways, then it becomes the curious case of, as we say in Latin *"auribus teneo lupum"* - holding a wolf by the ear: if you let go, wahala, if you hold on too, wahala. That's not to say some folks don't succeed, several do, through extreme discipline, ignoring systemic bias, forming the right relationships and taking advantage of the right opportunities, whether created or existing – some do succeed.

But for many others too, who have not been successful in the West and wish to return to Africa, there is the self-imposed pressure of thinking *"Can I display the kind of status that is expected of one who is returning from the West?"* Well, I often ask – who defines your status? Is it the material possessions or the mind to create the material comfort that matters? But it's real, people make their relocation *(or not)* decisions based on what they feel others might think about them. If you ask me, it shouldn't count.

What some might find interesting is, Africans' expectations of those returning from the West is gradually fading, if it has not already faded away completely. I spend half each year in Africa and believe me, cars like Mercedes, BMWs, Jaguars, Hummers, you name it, appear in Africa in the same months they are released in Europe and America. People in Africa now eat leisurely breakfasts, lunches or dinners in plush hotels. Africans can afford to buy tickets and make reservations for holidays outside their native countries. They have access to the latest technology. And it may surprise you to know that some Africans in the West, cannot even get a handle on these. So, yes, although it may not all be rosy, I frankly do not think the *"Lavish Expectations"* once placed on the returnee African still largely exists.

We can find many reasons to remain in the West: things work, education for our kids is world class, the advantages of being closer to early forms of technology, you can connect to the rest of the world better from here, there are laws that function, corruption is minimal *(I think that is a misconception, by the way)*, we can make money here to use back home *(and the opposite is true too, you'll be amazed)*, the health system works here. Of course, these decisions get harder once dependents come into the picture.

And there are equally good reasons for many to return home: there are equally world class private schools and health facilities, most technologies have no physical barriers globally and are accessible even in Africa just as they are in the West, the excellent all-year round weather, the good food, closeness to and support of close family, Africa is becoming *"the next big thing"* and with the right skills and mindset, one can make an impact, it's a less pressurized society, the world is coming to Africa, no racism or discrimination - I could go on and on, but you get the picture.

In all honesty, the decision really does come down to making a choice between two worlds — one in which you feel at peace but in which you equally must put in maximum effort to get results;

and one in which you feel alien no matter how hard you try to fit in, but in which even your tiniest efforts can be rewarding and where life and bureaucracy is largely predictable. It really is a choice between sanity versus vanity, spirituality versus worldliness, opportunity versus possibility, family versus individuality – each has a value to be gained and lost, each has a price to be paid. At the end of the day, one is Home, the other is Not.

This used to be someone's story. It is probably a story someone is wading through now and to others, it may be their battle in times to come. For me, this was my Afro-London Wahala!

Thank you so much for reading my book – it means a lot to share in my journey.

If you have enjoyed it, do leave me a review here on Amazon, so that others can be inspired to read it too.

Oh, and do share your favourite chapters

with an amazon link on Facebook!

You'll get a lot of hits!

AUTHOR'S OTHER WORKS

Title: **Is This Why Africa Is?** (E-book & Paperback)

Description: I ask all the questions about Africa that nobody else will. Deep, profound questions

Availability: Amazon & Kindle

Link to View: http://goo.gl/ecRMig

Title: **Doing Business with God** (E-book & Paperback)

Description: 60 shocking biblical principles for extraordinary leadership, business and politics.

Availability: Amazon & Kindle

Link to View: http://goo.gl/ecRMig

Title: **100% JOB INTERVIEW SUCCESS** (E-book & Paperback)

Description: A simple, straightforward guide to passing every job interview you attend.

Availability: Amazon & Kindle

Link to View: http://goo.gl/ecRMig

Title: **Ask and You Shall Marry** (E-book & Paperback)

Description: A Diary Of 303 Questions to Choose and Ask from Before Marriage

Availability: Amazon & Kindle

Link to View: http://goo.gl/ecRMig

Title: **The Graduate's Companion** (E-book & Paperback)

Description: 7 Vital questions ever graduate needs to answer before graduation. Things the will never teach you in

Availability: Amazon & Kindle

Link to View: http://goo.gl/ecRMig

ABOUT THE AUTHOR

Marricke Kofi GANE is a gifted African Author, Philosopher and Public Speaker. His writings carry real depth, are highly motivating yet challenging every non-progressive status quo. He displays dexterity of mind and a strong balance between his Christian roots and the reality of living in today's world. Discover for yourself, all that his writings stand for - to dare, to motivate, to impact!!

Email:
marrickegane@hotmail.com ; mkg@marricke.com
Website:
www.marricke.com
Skype & Twitter:
marrickegane; @marrickegane
Facebook:
www.facebook.com/marricke.gane ; www.facebook.com/
MKGspeaks